Landscape is the surface on which memory takes hold and sends downs its roots. To fully understand a place—beyond its geographical features—we need to listen to the stories of those who have lived there. This project is an attempt to preserve both a place and a narrative. A landscape is enduring but fragile. Wetlands, habitats, and open spaces vanish without stewardship. A narrative is fragile but enduring. Stories exist in our memory and remain alive only as long as we are willing to listen to them. Both play a crucial role in each other's survival and share a common goal: the preservation of a sense of place.

—BBS

Sheepscot Valley Conservation Association
Newcastle, Maine

AND THAT'S THE WAY OF IT
A Maine Village Life
1907–2002

Bird B. Stasz

Photography by Leah W. Sprague

SHEEPSCOT VALLEY CONSERVATION ASSOCIATION
624 Sheepscot Road, Newcastle, Maine 04553
207–586–5616 • www.sheepscot.org

First edition: December 2005

ISBN-10 0-9773151-0-X
ISBN-13 978-0-9773151-0-9

All proceeds from book sales benefit the Sheepscot Valley Conservation Association

Designed by Leah W. Sprague, Newcastle, Maine
Historical photographs compiled by Leah W. Sprague
Digital services by Noah Krell, Pure Photographic Goodness, Portland, Maine
Book production managed by Tilbury House, Gardiner, Maine
Copyediting by Barbara Diamond, Litchfield, Maine
Printed at Maple Vail, Kirkwood, New York, on acid-free paper with 50 percent
recycled content.

Cover photographs:
Sheepscot Village, photograph by Leah W. Sprague
Inset: Dorothy and a sheep in the Dow pasture, summer, 1920. From the
collection of Mary Ann and John Vinton
Title page spread:
Geese Over the King's Highway, photograph by Leah W. Sprague.

In memory of Jeffrey Douglas Raub, M.D.
1950–2004

Table of Contents

JAYBER CROW, THE NARRATOR of Wendell Berry's lyrical novel by the same name, at one point in the story reflects on his own life and his understanding of the passage of time. "Back then at the beginning, as I see now," he says, "My life was all time and almost no memory.... And now, nearing the end, I see that my life is almost entirely memory and very little time." Like Bird Stasz's remarkable Dorothy Carney Chase of Maine, "narrator" of this rich tale, Jayber Crow stops time with his clear memory and rich saga of his life and the stories of his community.

I can see Dorothy Chase, seated there at her window overlooking the Damariscotta River, re-imagining for Bird Stasz all she once lived and knows and wants to preserve through her story. Her story, it seems, just called for someone to be there and listen. Someone has to listen in order for the story to be told and heard, and we are blessed that Bird Stasz knew as much to do so. When Stasz and Chase met, what began—and what flourished— was a collaboration of remembering and telling made possible by their mutually dependent roles of talker and sympathetic listener. This collaboration opens a doorway for all of us to enter the life and the world Dorothy Chase recreates through her energetic and humorous narratives.

The remembered life must always be seen as something of an invention, a creative act. This by no means discounts the truth; in fact, the construction of the story may deepen the authenticity of experience, may make us feel the emotional truth all the more clearly. I'm reminded of the writer Harry Crews, who in the introduction to his memoir of his South Georgia life, *Childhood: A Biography of a Place,* begins with an admission and an exploration of the nature of memory. "My first memory is of a time ten years before I was born," he writes, "and the memory takes place where I have never been and involves my daddy whom I never knew." He knows what his memory knows because he comes from a place where, he says, "nothing is allowed to die in a society of storytelling people." And, he admits, what is told by those who carry the stories on "is colored and shaped by those who bring it." Likewise, nothing dies in the remembered life and landscape of Dorothy Chase as she brings forward forever the texture of her Maine life, lived well in an earlier time. While it's the past she remembers, her telling locates her story very much in the present.

Bird Stasz has collected, edited, and delivered to us a book of the same nature, a book of Dorothy Chase's life stories, selected through collaboration with Chase, true in all their humor, darkness, and frankness. From her seat in the Chase Point Assisted Living Center in Maine, Dorothy Chase creates a stage on which she presents her narrated life, a life we hear about and come to know through her friend many years her junior.

"Before I met you I had a life," Chase says to Stasz somewhere near the beginning of their time together, suggesting she almost sees her role more as teller than one who is still engaged in the act of living. But through the telling she lives all over again, affirming her place not only "back then" but in the moment of her telling. While telling about the life she lived and finding relevant connections to her place in the here and now, she gives new life to our understanding of local Maine culture.

Chase talks about a world of rural Maine that no longer exists except in the remembered and imagined cultural landscape of her stories. And then, through this book, the places exist again, in the minds of us, the readers and listeners. That magical process—from her memory, through her playful stories grounded in history, and then on to us—reconstructs what once seemed gone, invisible, forgotten.

"I have had a good old life." she tells Stasz toward the end of her story. "It is amazing what can go on in a life." Chase's sharp recall and wit make even the most ordinary happenings seem "amazing." "I don't have any regrets," she says. "I have had some disappointments—everyone does. But I don't have any regrets at all." No one who pulls a chair up next to Dorothy Chase and hears her story will have any regrets either.

Tom Rankin
Center for Documentary Studies at Duke University

Oldest known photograph of Sheepscot, circa 1885
IVAN FLYE COLLECTION

Acknowledgments

I WISH TO THANK the many people and organizations that helped to make this project possible. I am indebted to Wells College for a sabbatical leave that provided uninterrupted time to work, and to the Center for Documentary Studies at Duke University for allowing me to spend a wonderful year. Particularly I would like to thank Barbara Lau and Tom Rankin for their encouragement, reading of various drafts, and the time spent over coffee in conversation. Thanks goes as well to my department chair at Elon University, Deborah Long, for her encouragement and support. Also to Dianne Ford at Elon University for her work in locating elusive references, as well as the many reference librarians at the New England Historical and Genealogical Society in Boston, the Maine Historical Society in Portland, the Redwood Library and Athenaeum in Newport, the Rockefeller Library at Brown University in Providence, and the Skidompha Library in Damariscotta. I am most grateful for the dedication and efforts of Nancy Hartley, who sifted through the wills, deeds, and newspaper articles that helped anchor and flesh out so many of the mysteries alluded to in Dorothy's stories.

I wish to thank Jeff Raub, in whose memory this book is dedicated. Without Jeff, I never would have met Dorothy. Thanks also to Jennifer Bunting at Tilbury House for her advice, beautiful production, and coaching. Her patience and wisdom are much appreciated.

Thanks also to Leah Sprague for the beautiful images and for being such a willing partner in this project. To Sue Ellen Thompson, longtime friend, a large note of deep gratitude for reading the manuscript with such care—you have been a friend for the journey. Thank you also to Lee Smith and Memory Holloway for reading, encouraging, and supporting the project. I simply could not have done it without them. Finally, thanks to the generosity of those who made the book possible and to my family—Tom, Meghan, Jeff, and Bushy, whose patience, good humor, and encouragement are a great gift.

Dorothy Carney Chase
COLLECTION OF MARY ANN AND JOHN VINTON

Introduction

DOROTHY CARNEY CHASE was one of a kind. She was born in a snowstorm in Sheepscot, a village in Midcoast Maine, in 1907. On the day she was born, Dorothy was already an "old-timer." Her family had come to the village in the 1800s and had prospered there for generations. Like the tidal waters, the marshes, and the graveyard, she and her family were simply part of the landscape.

Dorothy was one of those rare individuals whose memory kept pace with her life span. At ninety-five she was sharp as a tack, slightly cranky, and notoriously independent, despite being wheelchair-bound. She hated reporters, telemarketers, and lazy people, and was quick to tell you so. But she was a consummate storyteller. Delivered in her rapid-fire style, Dorothy meted out lean narratives with flawless timing. Her stories cover the full range of human experience. Taken in aggregate, they paint an intimate portrait of New England village life and offer a parallel history that dates back to the American Revolution. More to the point, they represent the capacity of narrative to preserve that which has otherwise vanished. Dorothy was keenly aware that the village she grew up in and the people she had known existed now only in her memory. Like many places along the Maine Coast, Sheepscot had been "discovered"; gentrification, mobility, and wealth had forever altered the landscape and the definition of what it meant to be local.

Serendipity introduced us, and I spent a year listening

to Dorothy, taping her stories, and researching the appropriate background information. It was the last year of her life, and she knew it. Moreover, she had things to say and people for me to meet—not the least of whom were "the neighbors." These stories cover a startling amount of ground, defining and illuminating the larger issues of life—from success, education, and fair play to birth, belligerency, and death. They are a mix of dark and light, and their characters range from her sharply drawn grandfather, "Squire Carney," to the inhabitants of a small African-American community that remains a mystery to this day.

Dorothy wanted me to understand what it was like for families to know one another for generations, despite their troubles and idiosyncrasies. Stories—constituting social memory, providing commentary on behavior, archiving events, and reflecting a flexible version of the truth—are what held families together. They were embellished with bits of fact and fiction, creating a seamless transition from history to hearsay and back again.

In addition to preserving the past, Dorothy used stories to organize the present and to convey her thoughts on dying and what is important in life. When I asked her about the role of religion, for example, she responded by telling me a story: "It has dropped out of my life completely. It is interesting, though...." From there she launched into a very funny life review of all the different Protestant denominations to which she had belonged, concluding with the admonition, "I think what matters is how you live and to tell the truth."

It would be easy but unfair to Dorothy to cast this work in the warm and fuzzy glow of nostalgia for times gone by, or to present it as the ramblings of an old lady in an assisted-living facility. What Dorothy offers us is an opportunity to understand a piece of the historical record as mediated by personal narrative, allowing us to enter into a conversation with the past. Rather than telling stories entirely about herself, she told stories about people, places, and events as a way of explaining and preserving that which she felt was slipping away. She took pains to select only the best stories, the ones that were the most compelling and that offered the richest possible perspective. She could barely write because of her arthritis, but she spent hours jotting notes on scrap paper to remind her of the stories she would relate on my next visit. At the same time, she understood that a life consists of more than a series of events. "It is like the French and Indian stories and then the Revolutionary War stories and the Civil War stories," she once said. "You may have a history book, but that's all you've got."

This work is divided into seven chapters that are roughly chronological. Each chapter begins with Dorothy and ends with commentary, queries, and historical notes. Dorothy's stories are based in fact, and much of that information is supported by the endnotes, which offer a third view of the same landscape and add depth and historical background to the narrative.

As a final note, Dorothy's narrative approach to life

spills over into other areas of discourse. As we listen to Dorothy, we hear how narrative makes life and memory possible. The uniqueness of her experience translates to the experiences of others in a variety of settings from classrooms to community centers, from the academic to the public. Dorothy offers us the possibility of mutual conversations across time and circumstance, conversations that could not take place otherwise.

E. Joseph Leighton photograph, collection of W. H. Bunting

AND THAT'S THE WAY OF IT

Looking east over the Dyer River

Chapter One

YOU MUST BE THE ONE
Finding Dorothy and Sheepscot

I first met Dorothy quite by accident. I got her name from a friend of mine, Jeff Raub, who was the new emergency room director of a small hospital in Bangor, Maine. He had only been in town for a few months, but he was gregarious by nature and chatted up anyone who would listen. He knew of my interest in elderly women and mentioned it during a conversation with one of his attending physicians. Her response was that, of course, I should interview her mother. I had received suggestions like this before, and although Dorothy was in the right group—women over ninety— she was a little outside the scope of my current project, which dealt with New England women and community service. But she was nearby in an assisted-living facility, and an afternoon's conversation with anyone over the age of ninety is always interesting. If nothing else, I thought, our meeting would produce a tape that I could give to her family, a memento of her voice and the pleasant after- noon I had spent with her.

I phoned Dorothy's daughter, Mary Ann, to talk about the interview. She warned me that Dorothy was not enamored of reporters or telemarketing calls. Her hearing wasn't great, and she would probably slam the phone down if she weren't forewarned that my call was coming and that my motives were not suspect. Mary Ann had heard from the new doctor in Bangor that I had an "okay" reputation. I wasn't from the little village of Sheepscot, where Dorothy and generations of her family had been born, but at least I was from Maine, and talking to Dorothy would help the family preserve what she knew. "She is one of a kind, a vanishing breed, and she is full of stories," Mary Ann said of her mother. "We gave her a tape recorder, but she won't use it. She has good days and bad days, but it is important to get to her soon—before she is gone or forgets."

We talked a little longer about the kinds of questions I might ask and how the interview might proceed. I said that I was particularly interested in Dorothy's memories of growing up, and that I would steer away from deeply personal questions. I had learned years ago that women in their nineties, particularly if they're from New England, reveal personal information sparingly. When confronted with a question they'd rather not answer, they're likely to experience a sudden attack of "the vagaries" in which the conversation drifts off to other topics or dissolves into silence while they examine an infinitely interesting point in the distance. We set up a date, and Mary Ann promised to alert her mother that I would be coming to see her.

The day of my first interview with Dorothy was one

of those marvelous August days in Maine when the sky is cloudless, the sea sparkles, and the wind out of the northwest is heavy with the tart smell of seaweed and balsam. The light falls across the landscape with a clarity that is almost painful. It always reminds me of looking through freshly washed windows, and I half believed that if I flicked my fingers in the air, it would ping. Driving into Damariscotta, I decided to make my visit a quick one, as the weather was so fine it seemed a shame to spend any time at all indoors. With that in mind, I arrived at Chase Point Assisted Living Center early and found my way to Dorothy's room. I knocked on the door, and a sprightly voice, with a chuckle behind it and full of the sound of Maine, said, "Come in, come in."

I opened the door to find Dorothy sitting in a chair by the window, looking out over the Damariscotta River's tidal marshes and bird life. The view was superb, and it was obvious that she spent a lot of time there. Without missing a beat, she beckoned me into the room: "Come in dear, come in, you must be the one." She patted the seat beside her and said, "Sit right down here. Now what is your name and what are you doing?" The questions and commentary began in rapid fire. "You know I don't hear well," she said. Her thin hands immediately flew up to adjust her hearing aids, and she tilted her head toward me.

Physically, Dorothy Carney Chase was a paradox. On the one hand, she gave the appearance of being tiny and frail; on the other, she was so full of life it seemed she might take flight at any moment. On this day she was dressed, as usual, in a flowered housecoat that covered her knees and fell to the floor. Her hair was gray and in tight "beauty parlor" curls all over her head. When she smiled, her eyes crinkled and her eyebrows shot up, and I knew that I was in the presence of someone who laughed often and was vitally engaged in the world around her. There was nothing "old" about her, and yet she was wheelchair-bound, in her mid-nineties, and clearly approaching the end of her life. Her world was restricted to her chair, the window, her view of the tidewater, and her amazing memory.

Dorothy was clearly interested in my recording equipment, and as I got out the microphone, she chuckled and eyed it with a degree of skepticism. "'What happens if I start swearing—will you record that, too?" She laughed uproariously. "I asked my son-in-law, John, if it was okay to say the names of real people in my stories. I don't want to hurt anyone, but it won't make much sense if I don't use their names—besides, most of them are dead." Dorothy saw both humor and irony in being the last person to hold so many memories.

I spent two and a half hours with Dorothy on that first day and ran through tape accordingly. Interspersed with her stories were visits from her daughter and son-in-law, from staff at the assisted-living center, and from a cat—which sent her rummaging in her side table for catnip. There were discussions about ordering from a catalog, and the phone always seemed to be ringing.

Through it all, Dorothy kept telling stories. As I walked out the door, exhausted, I knew I would be back the next day regardless of the weather.

I got in the car and headed toward the village of Sheepscot. The only thing I knew about it, despite having driven through it at least a hundred times, was that it offered a way to avoid the relentless summer traffic that backed up from the bridge in Wiscasset. By turning right off Route 1 at Oliver Wendell Holmes Construction Company, now the site of Midnight Oil, I had often escaped being hung-up for hours trying to head south towards Portland. All the locals knew of this shortcut, and it had engendered moments of extreme smugness as

This year's lambs at Two Rivers Farm

miles of cars, gleaming in the sun, appeared in my rear-view mirror.

From June to September every year, thousands of people flock to the coast of Maine to participate in "The way life should be," as advertised on the sign at the Maine–New Hampshire border, only to find that instead, they are bogged down in traffic of urban-rush-hour proportions. Long lines of cars are loaded with camping gear, cranky children, panting dogs, and irritated parents whose enthusiasm for the annual summer pilgrimage to the shore is rapidly diminishing. The taste of lobster hardly seems worth the effort.

The village of Sheepscot lies five miles upriver from Wiscasset. A travel magazine might portray it as "picturesque," "quintessential New England," or any of those other terms that are so often used to describe a place about which the writer knows very little beyond well-known geographical features or architectural landmarks with little signs indicating that famous people wrote or slept there. But these symbols of celebrity status are hard to come by in small towns like Sheepscot, where the business of life has continued almost unnoticed by the rest of the world.

Sheepscot doesn't have outstanding man-made landmarks, just a few hard-to-find historic markers. In fact, the defining characteristic of Sheepscot is a bridge that crosses the Sheepscot River, linking Newcastle and Alna. The river is tidal, and depending on the time of day, great expanses of mud and marsh are exposed. Blue herons fish the shallows and, when startled, rise out of the sea grass like gray ghosts, squawking at each other in their smokers' voices. The river looks calm at high tide, but contains a treacherous piece of water that is deceptive and deadly. You certainly wouldn't know any of this by looking at it. The water seems harmless enough, unless you happen to be there when the tide turns and the reversing falls appear out of nowhere, forming deep, swift pools with flecks of sea foam on top, like whipped cream on cocoa.

From the middle of the Sheepscot River bridge looking downstream, there is a long expanse of easy, flat water winding through a valley that is a patchwork of fields and evergreens. A few houses dot the landscape, but it is still relatively rural. There is nothing to indicate that the Sheepscot River extends all the way to the ocean and at one time connected this little village to the much larger ports of Portland and Boston and, from there, to the Far East, Africa, and Asia.

Having kayaked the "backside" of the Sheepscot River, I know how easy it is to feel that you are a world away. The estuaries and backwaters twist and turn, full of bird life, otters, and fishers. There is the occasional island camp, a dock now and then, but in general, it is a quiet place that could not seem further from the summer activities so alluringly laid out in brochures and magazines.

Sheepscot does not have a main street lined with cute shops, restaurants, or quaint inns. In fact, it barely has a main street at all, except for the bridge and the "King's Highway." Unlike many coastal communities— Camden or Boothbay, for example—Sheepscot is not a tourist destination, at least not yet. It is virtually impossible to tell by driving through it what went on here, and more difficult still to figure out what Sheepscot meant to the families who lived here and called it home. The heart of the place is not easily discovered.

There are a few clues to be found in the local graveyard, which sits high on a hill just past the second of the village's two churches, one of which is Methodist and the other Congregational. Since there is only one graveyard, everyone winds up in the same place, regardless of church affiliation. I guess, after a point in time, denomination does not matter. It is located on a slope above the river, and the choice plots are either high up, with a good view, or down low, out of the wind. A number of ship captains are buried here, most of whom had worn out and outlived several wives, their stones scattered around their husbands' like leaves on the grass.

There are grave markers made out of slate and hand cut with dates that go back to the early 1700s. The names are of strong Scottish, Irish, and English ancestry, such as Chase, Carney, Marsh, Farnsworth, Cargill, and Glidden. But beyond their names, dates, and brief epitaphs, the stones are silent. There are a number of families with several generations buried here. Clearly the early residents of Sheepscot came early and stayed late. They were "of this place" for the duration of a lifetime and for generations to follow.

A small part of the cemetery is set aside for paupers.

Their gravestones are different: smaller, but of good quality white marble and hand-lettered. Two of them read,
"Unknown Infant" and "Unknown Man," both dated
1935. They are side by side, tucked away in a corner
under an old tree nestled in a drift of leaves from past
autumns. It is likely that these two were transients who
died of exposure or drowned in the river. They might not
even have been related, but the shared date and their
position together indicates that they had some connec-
tion. The inhabitants of Sheepscot took death and the
poor seriously and marked the passing of everyone, even
total strangers.

Up until 1971, individual towns in Maine were
responsible for the poor and infirm. In places like

Traffic jam, Sheepscot style

Sheepscot, where everyone knew everyone else, residents who fell on hard times had the dubious distinction of being listed in the annual town report as well as being taken care of by their neighbors. This practice of public disclosure went on until well into the twentieth century; it was no secret, therefore, who was receiving public assistance, how much, and for what reasons. The amounts ranged from two dollars to several hundred, all meticulously recorded and published yearly. The annual reports list payments for medical expenses for "tramps" and coffins for the public graveyard, as well as the school budget and bridge repair.[1] Most of the paupers are named, and their gravestones reflect the meticulous

Looking up the Sheepscot River

attention paid to local finances. Only last names and the year of death were etched on the stones, because it would have been too expensive to do more.

If I were going to spend more time with Dorothy, I would need to know more local history. From a trip to the library I learned that Sheepscot had been settled a long time ago. The first white European inhabitants were probably the Dutch, who arrived around 1607. A steady progression of settlers followed. The river was protected and made for an easy thoroughfare to the sea and the surrounding coast; lumber, fish, and game were plentiful. An early description reads, "It is beautiful tillage land; the surface being scarcely broken, by either ledge or rock that

Looking up the Dyer River

could not easily be removed. It was beautiful for situation, being almost surrounded by waters which were well stored with fish, particularly in the spring time, when the shad and salmon, and alewives[2] ran in vast quantities, and were easily taken. Above them too, oysters were found in considerable quantities. The forests abounded with game, and extensive marshes were near where they could cut hay for cattle."[3] To the newcomer's eye, Sheepscot must have seemed like the Garden of Eden.

In a case of colonial sleight of hand, the vast riches of the Sheepscot Valley were secured by the new colonists through a series of land sale agreements with the Native American population, and the new owners were John Mason, the Widow Gent, and Nicholas Manning. John Mason, an exceedingly enterprising fellow, arrived from Gravesend, England, on the *Philip* June 20, 1635, and married Mary Gent, the widow's daughter. Madame Gent's husband, John, a fisherman who was "cast away" at sea, had left his wife and family in Sheepscot the farm which he had fortuitously obtained from the Indians. Additional deed transfers occurred so that when all was said and done, the settlers' combined parcels formed a tenderloin of land approximately five miles long by a mile and a half wide—a bargain by any standards.

The architects of the land transfer managed not only to secure the land for themselves, but also to change the names of the original "owners" to better suit their needs, egos, and deed requirements. The January 20, 1652, deed is a transfer from "Robinhood, Dick Swash, and Jack Pudding to John Mason and his heirs, executors, administrators or assignees.[4] In a footnote from an 1847 publication of the Maine Historical Society, Robinhood is also known as Mohotiwormet and Dick Swash as Obias—both Native Americans. The names chosen by the English colonists were not without reference: Robin Hood (in the deed spelled Robinhood) is the main character in a series of folktales and ballads that date back to the Middle Ages, being an outlaw who was against the church. Jack Pudding is the name of an old and popular folk dance, also known as the Merry Andrew. Dick Swash was a nickname for Richard Cromwell, the incompetent and arrogant son of Oliver Cromwell, who managed to bankrupt England and was sent to live in Europe for many years. In short, the names chosen for the original occupants of this valuable and fertile territory, referred to in the early historical texts as "native lords of the soil," were hardly complimentary.

By 1664 the Duke of York, through the largess of the King of England, found himself with most of Sheepscot and the surrounding area as a land grant under his control. He established the first civil government at a meeting held at the home of John Mason. The new settlements were renamed New Dartmouth and New Castle, after their counterparts in England, and Sheepscot, which was the Abenaki word for "Many Rock Channels."[5]

Animosity between white colonial settlers and Native peoples began in earnest in Sheepscot, as it did in most of

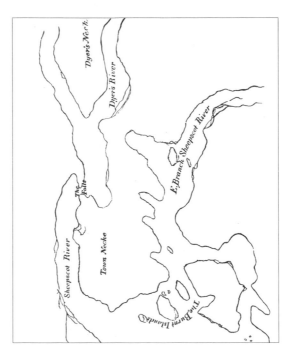

Above: Map by Nicholas Manning, seventeenth-century surveyor.
The East Branch of the Sheepscot River is now called the Marsh River.
MAP FROM *THE HISTORY OF ANCIENT SHEEPSCOT AND NEWCASTLE* (CUSHMAN)
Below: Present-day aerial view
COURTESY OF THE MAINE OFFICE OF GEOGRAPHIC INFORMATION SYSTEMS

New England, during King Philip's War (1675–76). Hostilities continued, with a series of intermittent truces, well into the 1700s. On the local level, changes in the ownership titles and status of lands fueled raids, massacres, and atrocities which were committed equally by both sides as each tried to maintain a foothold on the land they regarded as theirs. The problem was exacerbated by a profound difference in perspective on land use, devotion to property, and communal versus individual rights. As a result, the village of Sheepscot burned to the ground at least twice as settlers were attacked and retaliated.[6] At one point, a group of terrified farmers escaped down the river on an unfinished ship belonging to Sir William Phipps. Some went all the way to Boston and stayed there, while others returned. An account of this event appears in the writings of Cotton Mather.

The depth of the animosity between the settlers and Native peoples was played out in the person of Colonel James Cargill. Cargill, the second son of a surveyor, had a vicious hatred for "Indians" and showed no mercy, killing them whenever possible. While on a military expedition, he even went so far as to allow the shooting of a lone Native woman, Margaret Moxa, and her infant child. Moxa was a great friend of the settlers and had acted as a midwife and medicine woman, overseeing the births and illnesses of many. The settlers relied on her expertise, and her unjust and capricious murder raised a great hue and cry. Even the Penobscots, who up until this event were living in relative peace with the white population, sought retribution for her death.[7]

Colonel Cargill went to jail for two years but was acquitted without damage to his reputation as "killing Indians was no murder."[8] He went on to serve in the legislature and the general court and appears in town records as the person elected to transact public business because he was of "good reputation, judgment and prompt action."[9] All in all, the early years of settlement were far from tranquil. But despite its bloodthirsty and rocky start, the community of Sheepscot flourished.

The village grew on the foundations of what was known as the "Sheepscot Farms." These were the actual cellar holes of the very earliest settlers, chosen because of their advantageous location. Place names, which had originally come from geographical identifiers and Native American names, were changed to reflect the people who had lived there. Dyer's Neck, for example, was named after William Dyer, who bought his property from the Indians and farmed it until he was killed during one of the many Indian raids. Chase's Point was named for Captain Chase, one of Dorothy's relatives, who was tried for the crime of murder but acquitted. The "King's Highway," where most of Dorothy's family lived, was known as such because the original homeowners supported the crown. It became the favored location for houses because it occupied the height of land dividing the waters of the Sheepscot River from those of the Damariscotta—a long, flat ridge with good drainage and a commanding view of the waters below.

Shipyards sprouted along the river banks, using the huge timber supply from the surrounding forests to build vessels that would ply the great oceans of the world. It was rumored that the rings of the trees cut down numbered 150, clearly behemoths suitable for the masts of great sailing ships. These included fast, sleek vessels, captained by intelligent and able men, as well as tubby work boats that shuttled gear and supplies up and down the coast. A lumber mill went in above the tidal reversing falls, and a grist mill was soon grinding grain up on Mill Creek. There were blacksmiths, shopkeepers, farmers, seamstresses, postmasters, and all of the other accoutrements of early New England life. Sheepscot even produced veterans of the Revolutionary and Civil Wars. From its turbulent beginnings in the 1600s, it blossomed in the nineteenth and early twentieth centuries into a haven of civilized life. The duly elected public servants, who kept such eloquent and meticulous town reports, carried out the business of the citizenry, including a stand against liquor and a ban on breeding sheep and stray pigs.

Looking around Sheepscot on a sunny afternoon in August at the beginning of the twenty-first century, it is hard to imagine a thriving shipping industry with vessels built and launched above the reversing falls setting sail for the triangle trade, their captains men who now rest in the cemetery.[10] It is virtually impossible to find where wharves, shipyards, and mills might have been. There are still houses on the King's Highway, but they are mostly owned by people "from away," as out-of-staters are

A hot summer's day

referred to, or by newcomers who commute to work in Augusta and Bath. The commercial heart of Sheepscot is gone, which means it is impracticable to make a living here. There is no community public school within walking distance of the majority of the houses, nor is there a hospital, grocery store, gas station, or library. However, land development and speculation are as relentless here as anywhere else in coastal Maine. Prices have skyrocketed, and riverfront properties have become accessible only to the very wealthy.

Sheepscot, as it once was, now resides in only a very few places, in old newspaper articles, obituaries, and town records, and in the memory of one of its oldest residents, Dorothy Carney Chase.

I spent the better part of a year with Dorothy, flying back and forth to see her as often as I could. I taped her stories and then spent hours listening to her tell them over and over again, her voice drifting in and out of my ears as my fingers tried to capture in text what she had said and how she had said it. As I worked, I sent copies back to her, and when we were together again, she would add bits that she had forgotten or straighten out a crinkle in the tale, the way one might smooth the covers on a bed to set a room to rights and make it orderly and finished.

These are Dorothy's stories and, by extension, a portrait of life in a Maine village in the last century. They are about family, neighbors, work, place, and a worldview that is fading from our contemporary perspective. She delivered them with extraordinary skill and, from time to time, with a solid dose of Down East humor. Many of these stories reach back to a time before Dorothy's birth, but they are as integral to Sheepscot as the river under the bridge, the tide, and the empty cellar holes. Whether or not they are entirely accurate is irrelevant. They have been passed down to her from grandparents, parents, neighbors, and friends, and they represent the collective memory of a multi-faceted and peopled landscape. Dorothy acts as a bridge across time, geography, and experience. Without her, we cannot really "know" Sheepscot, nor can we imagine what it was like to grow up on this bend in the river, in Maine, at a time before the traffic jams and the highway signs.

This is also a story about coming to the end of one's life with a great deal to say, and relying on conversations with a total stranger to get it right. What follows is my attempt to understand what Dorothy's stories mean and, with her help, to navigate her life and the life of her village with honesty and grace. Much can be learned from her example.

On one of my many visits to Dorothy I said, half in jest, "Before I met you, I had a life." She laughed, winked, and nodded her head toward a huge black trunk on the floor of her room, full of old records, papers, and photos. "I bet you want to get your nose into there," she said.

And so I did.

1 *Annual Report of the Auditor of Accounts of the Town of Newcastle, Maine, for the Year Ending March 18, 1882* (Damariscotta: Dunbar Brothers, Printers), pp. 4–18.

2 Teresa Hineline, "Widows' Orders of Alewives Part of Town's History," *Lincoln County News,* 12 June 1993, pp. 1A and 8A. Alewives are a bony herring-like fish that were salted and stored through the winter. The alewives were so thick on the Sheepscot River that they turned the water black. In the middle of the eighteenth century a law was passed that widows were entitled to two free bushels of alewives per harvest. The law is still in effect; however, the alewife harvest has decreased dramatically and the smokehouses used for their preparation are long gone.

3 "Sheepscot," *Collections of the Maine Historical Society,* vol. IV (Portland: Maine Historical Society, 1856), p. 212.

4 William Willis, Esq., "Account of an Ancient Settlement on Sheepscot River," *Collections of the Maine Historical Society,* vol. ii (Portland, Maine: Maine Historical Society, 1852), p. 233.

5 Philip Rutherford, *Dictionary of Maine Place-names.* (Freeport, Maine: Bond Wheelwright Co., 1970). Fannie Hardy Eckstorm, *Indian Place-names of the Penobscot Valley and the Maine Coast* (Orono, Maine: University of Maine Press, 1974). Maine Studies no. 55 suggests that Sheepscot is in fact a combination of names from the Dutch and the Abenaki.

6 R. B. Fillmore Blind Canvasser, *Chronicles of Lincoln County* (Augusta, Maine: Kennebec Journal Print Shop, 1924), p. 69.

7 David Quimby Cushman,. *The History of Ancient Sheepscott and Newcastle including Early Pemaquid, Damariscotta, and Other Contiguous Places, from the Earliest Discovery to the Present Time* (Bath, Maine: E. Upton & Son, 1882), p. 141.

8 R. B. Fillmore Blind Canvasser, *Chronicles of Lincoln County* (Augusta: Kennebec Journal Print Shop, 1924), p. 71.

9 David Quimby Cushman, *The History of Ancient Sheepscott and Newcastle Including Early Pemaquid, Damariscotta, and other Contiguous Places, from the Earliest Discovery to the Present Time* (Bath, Maine: E. Upton & Son, 1882), p. 143.

10 The triangle trade ran from Portland to Charleston, South Carolina, where the vessels picked up cotton and transported it to Liverpool, England, where they took on manufactured goods and then returned to Portland. Another profitable trade route was from Portland to the Indies. Shingles and lumber went to Cuba and sugar returned for the distilleries in Maine.

Franklin L. Carney in his library, circa 1898
COLLECTION OF MARY ANN AND JOHN VINTON

Chapter Two

DIGGING UP GRAMPA
Establishing History

I have a story for you about burying Grampa," Dorothy begins. "Well, there was only one undertaker in my seven-year-old days in Sheepscot, and Grampa died. You know he was quite a dresser. He had starched shirt fronts, and he used to wear diamond shirt studs. Grampa had willed them to his youngest son, Clarence.[1]

Fred Harrington, the only undertaker we could have, told us that Grampa could be laid out in a coffin in his own home and then buried up in the cemetery. We didn't have to take Grampa anywhere, just leave him be. Fred told him [Clarence] that when he closed the coffin, he would take the shirt studs off, but he forgot. The whole family and most of the people from the surrounding towns came to the funeral. You know Grampa was called Squire Carney because he had his nose in everything in the town and everyone knew him and wanted to pay their respects.

Anyway, they took Grampa up to the cemetery and buried him. Then that night, Clarence asked Harrington for the diamonds, but he had forgotten, so he didn't know where they were. Those shirt studs must have still been on Grampa! That meant that two of the men in the village that my family knew had to go up to the cemetery and dig Grampa up and get the jewels. No one in the village was supposed to know. This was a big problem, everyone was out wandering around as it was a nice summer night and they couldn't sleep, and if they had seen someone digging up Grampa's grave there would have been a racket.

"So being the youngest, I heard from my sister Doris, who was a schoolteacher, what was going on. No one was supposed to know that Ernest Marsh and his brother Horace were up in the cemetery at midnight with lanterns digging Grampa up to get the jewels off his shirt for Clarence. Many years later when I was grown up, I went over to see Ernest and Maude Marsh. I said to him, 'Ernest,' I said, 'you had quite a time getting those jewels from Grampa.' You should have seen his face. Ernest was horrified that I knew. He said [imitating the sound of his voice], 'Dorothy, I didn't know anyone knew about that!' He was so afraid that someone would find him digging up Grampa. That is the story of Grampa's jewels.

"I have all kinds of stories about Grampa. He was something. Grampa Carney was very patriotic and always flew a flag every day. Most people did in Sheepscot back when I was a child. That was after the Civil War, not too far, and Grampa was a great man to have a flag around. Grampa didn't have a flagpole, because his house was a Victorian and there wasn't a flagpole that was high enough to fly above it. So he got a good-sized flag that he rolled up and pinned on a pole in the maple tree in the front yard of the house. It was a huge flag, and he rolled it out every morning and took it in every night. There was a driveway right next to the house, and he had a fence right along that line, and on his side he had buried in the ground wooden barrels. He saved the water off the roof in those barrels. That is the way they saved water in those days. He had beautiful gardens and flowers all over the place and he used the water from the barrels for that.

"Anyway, he had this big house on King's Highway, and his daughter Iva and her husband, who was a school principal, came every summer. In the fall, when they went back home, Grampa came up and stayed with us at

Grampa Carney's house on the King's Highway, circa 1889
COLLECTION OF MARY ANN AND JOHN VINTON

the farm. He was very elderly then and it wasn't good for him to try and live alone in that big house. Nevertheless, in the dead of winter, he would insist upon going down to see his house. He wore a nice felt hat and a nice-looking coat, and he always had a silk handkerchief in the tailpiece. I thought it was pretty nice, and he had a cane. He would want to go down and see his house, and Mother would have a fit. He would go into his kitchen and get some kindling and build a little fire in the stove. He would put his feet in and go to sleep. Then he would come home with a cold.

"My mother told him he couldn't go down there any-

Grampa Carney surrounded by his family at Echo Farm, 1900. Dorothy's mother is seated on the right; her father is seated on the steps, lower left.
COLLECTION OF MARY ANN AND JOHN VINTON

more unless he took one of us. He used to take me. We would stop at the store, and he would get me a bag of cookies. We went up to the house and he would get himself all stuffed up with his feet in the oven, and I would be eating cookies. When my cookies were gone, I would be ready to go home. So I used to wake him up and get him home. Mother made him take one of us so he wouldn't get a cold when he went down to visit his house.

"I remember my Grampa clearly as if it was yesterday. We had a ninetieth birthday party for him. I still have an invitation for it, and people came from everywhere to celebrate. Family came from New York, Boston, the Midwest, and all the local politicians, neighbors, and business people. It was a quite a gathering. His birthday

Carney and Goud Family Reunion, August 14, 1895
E. JOSEPH LEIGHTON COLLECTION, LINCOLN COUNTY HISTORICAL SOCIETY

got written up in the local papers. I found a picture of it.[2] The same picture was used in one of the historical pamphlets to show the kind of gatherings we used to have when whole families got together.[3] It was quite an event.

"There are so many stories about Grampa.... He always described himself as an abolitionist, a Methodist, and a member of the Temperance Society. He also liked cherry wine. He felt that it would keep him well. We kids had to go out on the paths between the different properties and get those wild cherries. We would have to go out and get them, and he would make wine out of it. He took a little bit every day; it was for medication—he didn't believe in anything else.

"I don't think young people like you understand Prohibition. Everyone in Sheepscot had a cupboard full of homemade things. There was pear wine that did this, and blueberry elixir that did that. Whenever anyone got sick, someone would hunt around in the cupboard and come up with a little bit of medicine. It was always homemade out of one thing or another that grew around.[4] That was what we did.

"Grampa was just like everybody else, he didn't have liquor around. But he felt he had to have cherry wine to keep him going. I remember going all over Sheepscot, picking those cherries. All of us kids did, and we brought them to Grampa. Then he did something or other to them—maybe added a little alcohol, for all I know—but he made his wine. That was his wine for medication and nothing else."

Dorothy ends on an emphatic note, "Yessuh," and settles back into her chair, squinting at me for a reaction. I don't disappoint her, as I find these stories engaging and totally plausible. Digging up Grampa speaks volumes about the times and the circumstances of life in Sheepscot in 1915. Shirt studs were worth more than the diamonds they held. The practice of "handing down" anchored an individual in terms of family, location, and narrative. Without the shirt studs, Grampa's passage to eternity would have been unremarkable. With them, it becomes an unforgettably funny story, and we both laugh uproariously for several minutes after Dorothy tells it.

Dorothy's memory is a gate through which time flows back and forth like the tide under the Sheepscot River bridge. She moves through the past deftly but at will, recounting tales that strike her fancy or convey a particular message without regard for chronology. Dorothy remembers her grandfather, who was born well before the Civil War, yet she is clearly comfortable in the present and engaged in the world beyond her room at the assisted-living center. She waits eagerly for her weekly news magazine, which she refers to as "Mr. Time Magazine." "Mr. Time Magazine" gets me more information in a week than anything I ever had," she tells me. When I was late for this interview and she knew I was flying up to see her, her immediate response to my arrival was, "I didn't want to turn on the TV, for fear you had been hijacked, just like in those towers."

As the stories about Grampa and the Carney clan

unfold, I periodically get lost and feel the need to bring order to her memories by imposing my own chronology and analysis. But in truth, I am astounded by how far back and forward her mind can reach. When I asked Dorothy the inevitable, "How did your family come to Sheepscot, Maine?" she replied, "You don't want to get that far; you want to come to places before you get there. So the first one you have to have is when I started coming to the United States."

She is an amateur genealogist, and her knowledge of family history is immense. The saga of the Carney clan rolls out of her memory in one long story filled with colorful characters that include privateers, Huguenots, scoundrels, kidnappers, and Revolutionary War heroes. When I ask how her family came to Maine, Dorothy reduces a complicated piece of history into a simple tale of love, land, and serendipity: "It was just a case, I like to think, of two sailors who came over on a boat and saw two pretty young French girls and decided to skip the boat they were on and to stay in this new settlement. They would give you a little piece of land and a little cupboard to live in. That was just the way of it. I don't know if that is true or not, but that is the way I like to think of it."

As Dorothy talks, I find myself sifting and shaping her family history so that I can place it in a broader context. After all, the history of her family is a mini-history of early colonial life, particularly New England. The characters in her stories are ordinary people, caught up in tumultuous times. From our vantage point, their experiences seem surreal but in fact, are not uncommon for the day and time. They illuminate a landscape and a mind set that is simultaneously commonplace and extraordinary. Clarisse Coleman, a talented young writer I know, once asked, "What is the difference between a string of anecdotes and a story that is close to the bone?"[5] I have no idea, but that is the task I am facing. I have to step away from the tape recorder to summarize and weave in bits of history from other sources before I can find my way back to Grampa, Dorothy, and the bridge over the Sheepscot River.

Dorothy is eager to tell me the story of how Grampa got his middle name. "Oh, yes," she says, "here's one. My great-grandfather, Daniel Carney, named my grandfather Franklin LaFayette Carney because [the French soldier] Lafayette came to be honored after the Revolution because he had helped so much. He [the Marquis de Lafayette] came back to Boston, and they had a big dinner party on the Common. An uncle held Grampa up as a baby and said, 'His name will be Franklin LaFayette.' The story goes that Lafayette acknowledged the uncle with a bow. So that is how that got into the family."[6]

Dorothy also tells the story of Josiah Wheeler, a great-great-grandfather who was a master carpenter and commanded a company of Minutemen, mostly skilled carpenters and joiners, at the beginning of the Revolution. At the request of General George Washington, they built the fort and the battlements on Dorchester

Heights. It is said that he got a sword for his efforts, but no one has seen it lately. Josiah also played a part in the Boston Tea Party.

"There is another family story that Grampa told. It seems that Josiah was acting strangely, and his wife was worried about him. It was December 16, 1773, and he was being peculiar all day. He was very late getting home that night, and his wife waited up for him. When he finally did get home, he sat down in front of her and took off his boots. Tea fell out, which gave a big clue to what he had been up to that night. His wife just swept it right into the fire, saying, 'do not touch the cursed stuff'."[7]

As we edge closer to Sheepscot, there is the story of Great-Grandfather Carney, who fell upon poor times and used his wife's money to pay off his debts. As Dorothy puts it, "Daniel Carney was doing a good West Indies business in Boston. He had been in business almost fifty years. He was an alderman, a banker, and a few other things. It sounded like he was doing all right when dog-gone, he lost his business. It was said that when Mary Wheeler's father died, she had inherited, it was thought, as much as eight hundred dollars in silver, yessuh. So he paid his bills with his wife's money and came down to Sheepscot and progressed from there. That is when Grampa came to Sheepscot, when he was six years old.[8] It was 1830."

Coming from Boston to Sheepscot, Maine, must have been a rude awakening for the Carney clan but especially for Mary, who had lived all her life in the bustling port city. She had been educated in private schools and was a member of the Handel and Haydn Musical Society.[9] In his section of the family genealogy, Grampa Carney, her son, describes his mother as someone who "had a beautiful voice and often wore satin slippers." One can only imagine what went through her mind as she, her nine children, and most of their household possessions were loaded onto a vessel that left Boston Harbor to slip Down East for the relative obscurity of the Maine Coast.[10]

The circumstances surrounding the arrival of the Carney family were not unusual.[11] With the Revolution barely a generation behind them and the Civil War yet to come, business was bad in Massachusetts, and Maine offered the promise of a new beginning. Maine ship captains connected their coastal villages to the rest of the world, and that meant opportunity. There was even a joke going around that you were more likely to see your neighbors in Singapore than on Main Street. Daniel had a brother in a small town close to Sheepscot and, as Dorothy says, "He had land from Dresden."[12] More importantly, he had a job. On April 14, 1830 Daniel Carney was appointed postmaster at Sheepscot, a position he would hold for the next nineteen years.[13]

In those days, Sheepscot was a busy place, much busier than now. The population was larger than one might think, consisting of 202 families, many descended from the original settlers. As Dorothy says, "In the old days, you were there forever and had grandchildren and great-grandchildren." Even as early as 1788, Sheepscot

The catch; fish weirs in the Sheepscot River,
looking west from Two Rivers Farm
E. JOSEPH LEIGHTON COLLECTION, LINCOLN COUNTY HISTORICAL SOCIETY

had wealthy residents such as Captain Robert Hodge, who died with an estate of £3,895, 4S, 10P. Among his many possessions were several cases of gin, valued at a pound each, one hogshead of rum at £10, and half ownership of the sloops *Ranger* and *Dolphin*.[14] The citizenry was a mixed lot of gentry, farmers, laborers, shipbuilders, and businessmen. There were people like Captain Goddard, described in his obituary as "a longtime resident of Sheepscot Bridge, well remembered by the elderly and middle-aged citizens as a finely educated man of elegant and courtly manners."[15]

The good soil along the river attracted prosperous farmers. The new toll bridge was in, replacing the ferry and making travel to the surrounding towns not only possible but relatively easy. Timber was plentiful, and there were shipyards above the falls on the river. In fact, when Daniel's affairs had been better he, along with a gentleman with the last name of Howard had completed the 130-ton schooner *Chariot* in 1825 and two years later, the 273-ton brig *Sabbatis*.[16] Both these vessels were built in the shipyard in Sheepscot and launched, along with others, at the bridge in the village. Also launched there was a little steamboat called *Morgan's Rattler*. She puffed up and down the river, slow and noisy but useful, carrying goods and people from Wiscasset to Sheepscot and back again. There was a thriving fishing industry and a brick-making business. Sheepscot wasn't Boston, but it was going to be home to Mary, her son Franklin La Fayette, and the Carney clan for years to come. In fact, it was a place that Grampa would take by storm.

In the family genealogy, Grampa Carney describes his beginnings in Sheepscot. "Going to Maine when six years of age, I had to put up with the three months' public school per annum, on Garrison Hill with an occasional private school and what I learned when quite young in the printing offices of the *Lincoln Patrol* and *Wiscasset Weekly*. This completed my meager education in school." He was also acutely aware of his responsibility to his parents and writes, "Whatever I could find for my hands to do, to help Father in his old age, I commenced to do for [him]."[17]

Despite his limited education, Franklin Carney was an ambitious and energetic man, and Sheepscot was clearly "his place." Dorothy often uses the phrase, "I took life and I lived it," implying an almost insatiable enthusiasm for experience and opportunity. The same could be said for Grampa. He was the quintessential self-made New Englander, and he had his finger in every pie in the village, from commerce to politics.

In 1847 he took over as postmaster.[18] This position led to offices as toll collector on the bridge, justice of the peace, selectman, and overseer of the poor. He was a director of the Wiscasset Bank and founder of the Mariners' Bank. Grampa was elected a member of the state House of Representatives from Newcastle and later served as a state senator for Lincoln County. He knew everyone from the governor of the state to the local fishermen. As Dorothy says about her grandfather, "He was

Celebration in front of the F. L. Carney store, June 22, 1894. The occasion: the "freeing of the bridge" from tolls. On the balcony, from left, are Dorothy's half-brother Richard and Uncle Clarence Carney.

COLLECTION OF MARY ANN AND JOHN VINTON

respected, everyone traded with him. He was honest. I have in his account books the names of the people who came and the women who did the washing. People came to the door and sold clams. He bought from everyone. It is all in there. He kept careful records his whole life. I could tell you how much it cost for him to live a year." His records, meticulously entered into small leather-bound ledgers in a fine hand, are so precise that they include the dollar a year that he gave as a birthday present to each of his grandchildren.[19] This attention to financial detail is not really about accounting practices as much as it is about establishing a reputation for honesty and integrity. Grampa was a man of his word; one only had to look at his accounts to know that.

Grampa Carney did not lack for business acumen, either. At the bridge, he opened a much-needed general store that provided basic necessities, from flour to boots to candy. Prior to this, Sheepscot residents had to travel to other villages, such as Damariscotta, to get staples. It was not an easy trip in a horse and wagon over rough roads. Meat and fish were still purchased directly from a peddler's cart that went around the village or directly from the local farmer or fisherman. In addition to providing a service to the citizenry of Sheepscot, the store

Schooner and tug leaving Jack's Wharf
E. JOSEPH LEIGHTON PHOTOGRAPH, COLLECTION OF DORIS LEIGHTON PIERCE

provided a gathering place and a center for swapping information, local gossip, and the news of the day.[20] One can surmise that it also kept Grampa Carney at the center of events in the village.

From commercial and civic ventures, he moved into the lumber and milling business as well as shipbuilding. He bought up lumber lots and sold wood to the Bath Box Works. Dorothy recalls, "He would buy them [the wood lots] up and the French Canadians used to come down with portable sawmills.[21] They set up camps, and when Grampa and Pa had business there, Louise and I would go visit. The kids would come to school with us in the village and my pal Louise and I would play with them. So when Pa had business, I got to go along and see how things were. I remember it well. The cabins were small, one per family, with bunks all around and a lot of people in just one room.[22] Because they traveled all the time, everyone had just a few things. I couldn't understand what anybody was saying because they were all speaking French, but Louise and I had a good time. Kids don't care about all those things, they just get along, I think. Anyway, once the lumber was cut, the scows would come up the river and the lumber would come down by horse and be loaded on the scows and sent to Bath."

Grampa writes with an element of pride about his shipbuilding ventures. "In 1880, I commenced building vessels, building and owning in part the following: the three-masted schooner *Annie B. Chase*, three-masted schooner *Isaac Osheton*, barks *F. L. Carney*, *Pleiades*, *Isaac*

Rich, Elwood Cooper, and *R. Murray, Jr.*"

The *F. L. Carney* was built in 1874. She was 138.1 feet overall, 32 feet abeam, and drew 18.73 feet. Her home port was actually New York, and her registered owner was R. Murray, Jr., who was a business partner of Grampa's. The *F. L. Carney* sank in a storm off Diamond Shoals on January 22, 1882, and went down with all hands except the ship's carpenter.

The Coast Guard reported the rescue. In an effort to set the record straight (a characteristic of the precision of the New England narrative), Captain R. J. Gill of the schooner *Watchful* wrote an irate article for the *Lincoln Record* in February of 1882 recounting a corrected version of the story. The article, entitled "More About the *F. L. Carney,*" goes into detail about the Coast Guard's inept handling of the incident.[23] Indeed, it was Captain Gill who rescued the lone carpenter, not the Coast Guard; the Captain believed that more lives could have been saved if the Coast Guard had been doing its job. The article ends with a tart reproach: "If they [the Coast Guard] are not to save life and property, then what is the use of them? If you will insert this in your very valuable paper, you will do something to have proper men at some of our needed stations." Grampa ended his shipbuilding career soon after this event and wrote, "I was always able to pay one hundred cents on the dollar and got out of shipping in time to save, I trust, with care, enough to last the little time I shall need money."

When I ask Dorothy more about her grandfather, she

holds out Sheepscot's town report for 1887. "You need to read this part, where Grampa scolds the residents of the town for wasting money." As the town auditor, F. L. Carney takes the residents of Sheepscot to task for incurring a debt for the narrow-gauge railroad. He writes, "That we have an elephant upon our hands no one disputes. Our only way seems to be to continue his feed until someone else wants him or the silver dollars of our fathers become so plentiful that he can pay his own bills. And trusting to Providence, he will not in the meantime eat us up. What measures the town Brethren, herewith I have no information to advise from." In a later report he writes, "We are now passing through the experience of gradually paying a debt we never should have contracted; yet, having done so, no honorable method remains but to meet it, as far as our ability will allow, as we agreed. The only questions open are how best to meet this unfortunate state of affairs, and can the town continue to bear to the end the great strain put upon her, or must some method be adopted to put to another time a part of this great debt?"[24] Other admonishments regarding civic pride and responsibility, financial integrity, and honesty appear in family stories and town reports. They are the cornerstones of Franklin Carney's personal philosophy and reflect the values of the day in Sheepscot. It is almost as if Grampa Carney established the standards by which the rest of the community was measured.

On a dreary afternoon in November, just after one of my sessions with Dorothy, I go to see Grampa's house and

Reversing Falls, 2005. Grampa Carney's house on the
King's Highway is visible to the right of center.

locate the maple tree in the front yard that had once held
his American flag. The house is large, stately, and beautiful, a testament to the craftsmen of the day and to
Grampa's success in life. I knock on the door to see if the
current owners will let me step inside and try to imagine
the man for whom their house was built, but no one
is home. Clearly Providence had smiled on Grampa,
although like most New Englanders, he undoubtedly
would have attributed his material success to his own
hard work and strength of character.

When I return, I question Dorothy once again about

the cherry wine—I am puzzled as to how one can simultaneously be a Prohibitionist and a winemaker. I am familiar with such old-time medications as Purena, which was about 90 proof. There is even an old song that goes, "Nobody drinks in this house, we all drink Purena." Obviously the line between drinking alcohol for pleasure and using it for medicinal purposes was a fine one, and I doubt that Grampa Carney was the only one who had crossed it on occasion. From the look on Dorothy's face when I bring up the subject, however, it is not worth pursuing.

This and other stories about Grampa illuminate a more flexible moral and political landscape than what can be found in history books or the public records. They also make Grampa a little less heroic and a great deal more human. It is difficult to imagine anyone today sending an army of little children out to gather wild cherries for an old man's "medicine."

1. Franklin L. Carney, Last Will and Testament, Lincoln County Vital Records, Wiscasset, Maine, 1878–1915, vol. 195, p. 532. Grampa Carney deeded "[my] diamond shirt studs, my gold watch chain, personal jewelry to my son Clarence. I also give him the organ piano and my covered rocking chair." Grampa divided his considerable real estate holdings equally among his surviving children—Clarence, Ada, and Franklin C., Dorothy's father. To his daughter Ada, he left, "all the wearing apparel, jewelry, and small personal things belonging to her Mother, my beloved Wife, to dispose of or to keep as her own as she pleases, except her Mother's Gold Watch and chain, which is given to Cecilia Ida Doe." The will is handwritten in an elegant and even script.

2 Dorothy Carney Chase, private collection: photographs.

3 Ava Chadbourne, *Maine Place Names and the Peopling of Its Towns* (Portland, Maine: Bond Wheelwright Company, 1957), p. 4.

4 Caryl de Trecesson and Carol Hansen. "Cordial Recipes." Retrieved 3/25/2003 from www.dragonbear.com/cordials.html. Making fruit cordials was common in New England, as it was in most of colonial America. Recipes dating back to 1550 can be found as "hand-downs" in the cookbooks of such colonial luminaries as Martha Washington. Many of these cordials had medicinal value and such hopeful names as "The Water of Life"—which, according to the label, "defendeth against all pestilentiall diseases, as against paulsie, dropsie, spleen, yellow or black jaundice for wormes in the bellye, and for agues be they hot or cold and all manner of swettings." Additional information on home remedies—specifically those grown in a typical Maine garden—can be found in G. Chase, *An Herbal of the 18th Century Gardens at Tate House* (Portland: National Society of the Colonial Dames of Maine, 1991).

5 Clarisse Coleman, writer's workshop, May 2002. Clarisse Coleman received her MFA in literary non-fiction from Bennington College. She is the author of numerous articles and is the 2001–02 recipient of the Writer's Fellowship from the North Carolina Arts Council. She currently teaches at Duke University.

6 This story is corroborated in Sydney Carney, *Genealogy of the Carney Family: Descendents of Mark Carney and Suzanne Goux, his Wife of Pownalboro, Maine, 1751-1903* (Boston: Photoduplication, New England Historic Genealogical Society). The Marquis de Lafayette did return to Boston for a gala hero's welcome and return. The dates and times fit with the birth of Grampa Carney, although if all else is correct, he was but five days old at the time of this great event. The description of Lafayette's visit to Boston is as follows: "August 24, 1824, at 9 o'clock in the morning a cavalcade of about 800 selected Boston citizens came to the dwelling of Governor Eustice where they took Lafayette in charge and conducted him to the city limits where the city authorities were awaiting to receive him. The mob on the road was so unruly that it took two hours to cover the two miles to Boston" (p.1). The caravan then went through the streets of Boston and under the civic arches on Washington Street, which was in the same neighborhood as the Carney household. A detailed and interesting description can be found in C. Browning, *The American Historical Register and Monthly Gazette of the Patriotic-Hereditary Societies of the United States of America,* September 1895–February 1896 (Philadelphia: Historical Register Publishing Company, 1896).

7 A very close rendition of this story appears in Francis Drake's, *Tea Leaves: being a collection of letters and documents relating to the shipment of Tea to the American Colonies in the Year 1773,* (Boston: A. O. Crane, 1884), p. CLXIX.

8 Sydney Carney, *Genealogy of the Carney Family: Descendents of Mark Carney and Suzanne Goux, His Wife of Pownalboro Maine, 1751–1903* (New York: Edward

Bierstadt. Photoduplication, New England Historic Genealogical Society, Boston, Massachusetts, 1915), p. 138. Grampa Carney wrote his own summary of his life and events and they appear under his name in the text.

9 J. Winsor, ed., librarian of Harvard University. *The Memorial History of Boston Including Suffolk County Massachusetts 1630–1880 in Four Volumes. The Last Hundred Years. Part II Special Topics* (Boston: James R. Osgood and Company, 1883). "The Handel and Haydn Society was founded in 1815 and was one of the first examples of music as independent from the Puritan Psalmody, a monotonous and barren music that was common throughout New England" (p. 418). The major performance of the Society was the *Messiah,* which was performed over seventy times between 1818 and 1880.

10 M. B. Sweetser, *King's Handbook of Boston Harbor* (Boston: Moses King Corporation, 1886). "As early as 1823, there was a regular line of steamers between Boston and Bath and thence to Boothbay, Camden, Belfast, Sedgwick, and Eastport" (p. 297). The steamships, even the early ones, are described as being fairly fast, commodious vessels with passenger accommodations at varying levels of luxury, from staterooms to steerage. The vessels made regular trips Down East for economical fares. The ships followed the coast, except for making overnight trips across the Gulf of Maine. After 1842, Captain Sanford established the Sanford Steamship Company, which remained in business, except for a brief hiatus during the Civil War, when most of his ships were commandeered by the Union Army. By 1882, the Sanford Steamship Company became the Boston and Bangor Steamship Company, which launched beautifully appointed state-of-the-art steamships that plied the waters of the New England Coast, bringing tourists and residents "Down East" in style and comfort for the reasonable fare of $4.50 round trip, Boston to Rockland. The steamship companies, in conjunction with the railroads, opened up the interior of Maine as well as the coast. The ships ran as far Down East as Frenchman's Bay and Bar Harbor.

11 J. Winsor, ed., librarian of Harvard University. *The Memorial History of Boston Including Suffolk County Massachusetts 1630–1880* (Boston: James R. Osgood and Company, 1883). Business, particularly the West Indian trade, was hard hit by the War of 1812. It is conceivable that Daniel Carney's fortunes did not recover in the postwar economic turnaround. Between 1810 and 1820, the taxable valuation of Boston went from $18,500,000 to $38,000,000. The new commodity that created something of an economic boom in the shipping industry was the exporting of ice to the West Indies and Europe. *The Boston Taxpayer 1821–1822* shows a Daniel Carney and shop on Orange Street in Boston with a sizable real-estate value of $900 and a personal evaluation of $1,000.

12 The Register of Deeds for Lincoln County, Maine, shows land transfers between

Daniel Carney and his brother William in Dresden beginning in 1825. Apparently Daniel preceded him to Maine and purchased various parcels of land, some of which he then sold to his brother William.

13 *Annual Report of the Auditor of Accounts of the Town of Newcastle, Maine, for the Year Ending March 18, 1882* (Damariscotta: Dunbar Brothers, Printers).

14 Captain Robert Hodge, "Inventory of the real and personal estate of Sept 20, 1788," *Vital Records,* Lincoln County, Maine, Wiscasset, Maine, vol. 4, pp. 247–54. This inventory is particularly interesting as it is referenced in D. Cushman, *The History of Ancient Sheepscot and Newcastle,* as including a slave as part of the inventory. However, there is no mention of this in the inventory on file at the courthouse.

15 "Capt. Goddard Not a Jonah," *Wiscasset Lilliputian,* February 7, 1885.

16 Deputy Collector Sidelinger, *Sidelinger List of Shipping Built in the Towns of Newcastle, Nobleboro, Damariscotta and Bristol* (Skidompha Library, Damariscotta, Maine). The schooner *Chariot* was built in 1825 by Carney and Howard. She received her register in New York March 21, 1826, and her rig was given as a brig. The schooner *Sabbatis,* also built by Carney and Howard, was registered in New York as well.

17 Sydney Carney, *Genealogy of the Carney Family: Descendents of Mark Carney and Suzanne Goux, His Wife of Pownalboro, Maine, 1751–1903* (New York: Edward Bierstadt. Photoduplication, New England Historic Genealogical Society, Boston, Massachusetts), 1915.

18 *Annual Report of the Auditor of Accounts of the Town of Newcastle, Maine, for the Year Ending March 18, 1882* (Damariscotta: Dunbar Brothers, Printers).

19 Dorothy Carney Chase private collection: ledger(s) of Franklin La Fayette Carney. The pocket ledgers of Grampa Carney span the adult and business years of his life. Each entry is carefully recorded in his fine hand and includes all manner of expenditures such as laundry services, repairs to his wagon, farrier expenses, and personal purchases—from shirts to buckets. The ledgers illuminate the daily economic life of a man of means in Maine in the late-nineteenth century.

20 Lew Dietz, *Night Train at Wiscasset Station* (Garden City: Doubleday, 1977). The role of the general store in New England villages is well documented but remains unique to a bygone era. These stores carried everything from boots to molasses and served as a center for the exchange of goods as well as for news, gossip, and amenities. General stores served as post offices, stage coach stops, occa-

sionally as inns, and almost always as a place for the rural people of the nineteenth and early twentieth centuries to escape their hardworking and often isolated lives.

Early storekeepers such as Grampa Carney were usually good businessmen and of good reputation. They were first and foremost good traders, as cash was often in short supply. It was not uncommon to barter sheep for buckwheat, fish for tackle, and shingles for molasses. The nature of the trade was critical. If the shop-keeper gave someone a "poor trade," his reputation would take a downward turn. If he was considered tough but fair, his reputation would rise.

21 Horace Beck, *The Folklore of Maine* (Philadelphia: Lippincott, 1957). The lumber industry in Maine went through four basic but overlapping phases. The first was the mast industry, which entailed the cutting of spars and masts for ships. The huge trees of early Maine were perfect as they were tall, straight, and plentiful. The second was the cutting of pine and spruce for lumber and finally pulp for paper. The lumber camps were the center of activity for the industry. It was here that the loggers lived and worked, often migrating from place to place. The portable lumber mills were brought down from Canada and set up on a contract basis. Life in the lumber camp was no picnic, as space was limited and the work hard and exceedingly dangerous. Lumberjacks were killed by falling limbs (known as widow-makers) and up-ended trees, and accidents were as common and predictable as sunrise. When families came along, the children would go temporarily to the local school until their fathers moved on to the next job. The nature of the work and the locations resulted in a self-contained world. The life of the lumber camp is replete with its own songs, stories, beliefs, and vocabulary. "Drivers" or "river hogs" were men who branded the logs and floated them downstream, "swampers" were those who cleared paths and made roads into the camps. The vocabulary of the logging camp included words like "slologan" (a stillwater pond or freshwater bay), "dry ki" (dead standing timber), and "puckerbrush" (low dense growth). Even words that seem common took on other meanings. The "deacon's bench" was a long pine slab in the middle of the lumber camp where individuals told stories or sang songs. As time went on and the lumber industry became increasingly more mechanized, the lumber camp disappeared and with it, this distinctive but difficult way of life.

22 Dorothy Carney Chase private collection: photographs of the lumber camp.

23 "More About the *F. L. Carney,*" *Lincoln County Record,* February 1882

24 *Annual Report of the Auditor of Accounts of the Town of Newcastle, Maine, for the Year Ending March 1887* (Damariscotta, Maine: Dunbar Brothers, 1887).

Dorothy Carney Chase
COLLECTION OF MARY ANN AND JOHN VINTON

Chapter Three

The "Beautiful Life"
Family and Farm

*I*t is an Indian summer afternoon in early October when I go to see Dorothy for our usual session. The light is softer than in August, and typical of Indian summer the days are mild and the nights chilly. On the tidal marshes the geese are on their way south and you can hear them calling to one another high up in the air. It is a reflective time of year and our time together seems to be growing shorter along with the light and the warmth. Dorothy, however, starts the afternoon in great humor.

"You know, I think I insulted Donna. Donna is the one that comes in and takes care of me. She came in and told me her name was Donna and I said, 'Oh, I can remember that—I had a horse named Donna!' But I couldn't remember her name when she came in a second time, so I had to ask her to introduce herself to [my daughter and son-in-law] Mary Ann and John. She said, 'Oh, you remember my name—you knew a horse named that!' We all laughed." And with that, Dorothy launches into the story of Donna the Horse.

"Burglars came in the night and smashed into the stable and stole Donna. They were up in the schoolhouse, which at the time was right near the Congregational Church. Nobody knew who they were. We thought that they might have been in prison and heard about Sheepscot from there. They came up to Sheepscot on the narrow-gauge[1] at dark. Even though no one in the village knew them, they knew that the schoolhouse had been heated and they could get in there and stay the night, because it was warm. While they were in there doing that, everyone went to bed and a blizzard came on. You know, snow and ice. It was a terrible night.

"Evidently they got in the woodshed and got the ax and came down to our farm after everything calmed down. It didn't take long to calm Sheepscot down in those days," Dorothy said with a laugh and sped on. "My folks could hear a noise in the barn. My mother was always telling my father to go out there because she heard something. They [the burglars] came to the barn, but no one could hear anything over this howling wind, and they took Donna. Lucky there were sleighs and a pung.

"Do you know what a pung is? It is like a Ford pick-up with no back end to it. A pung had a place to put your supplies. You didn't have a fancy cushion. So they came and took the pung and all the robes and furs they could find, and they chose Donna, harnessed her up, and then went out.[2] They took the back road to Damariscotta and got as far as the Mills when they decided to open a store. The robbers broke into J. Wilder Haggett's, which at the time was one of the largest and best-equipped general stores in this part of the state.[3] Well, they blew open the safe and took their loot. The wind was howling, and they were cold and everything. They covered themselves up and got back in the pung.

"Well, I don't know where they thought they were going, but they were getting out of Sheepscot and going further Down East. I suppose the railroad had something to do with their choices. Maybe they thought they could get away by picking up the railroad in some remote spot. I don't know. Well, they let Donna loose [letting Donna loose means that they just held the reins slack and let her find her own way] and the next time they looked up, they were coming into Damariscotta village with morning

Dorothy's sister Gladys with Donna at Echo Farm
COLLECTION OF MARY ANN AND JOHN VINTON

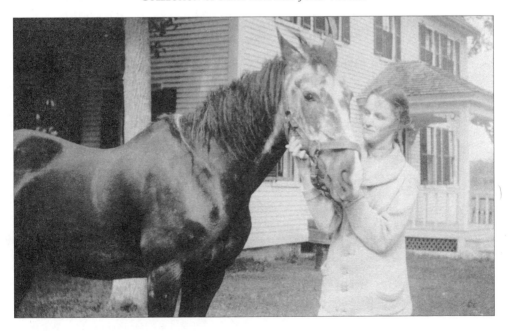

coming on. Donna knew the right-hand road, so she took it. They didn't want to get caught, and they knew that everyone would know the horse was lost, so they looked around and saw Wheeler's big barn. They thought that was a good place to hide, so they got out and took their loot and everything with them and let Donna go. I don't even think they turned her around, I think she just knew. You know, those two men crawled into the haymow.

"Well, my father got up in the morning at seven o'clock to feed the cows, and Donna whinnied to him outside the stable door. She had brought herself all the way home. The storm was so bad that she was covered with ice and sleet. She knew enough to go out and around the bad drifts in the road. She had come home all by herself, and she was calling to him from outside.

"She always whinnied to him. Whenever he went to the barn, she would talk to him. She was awful bright. I guess it was a nice breed. My mother said that the mother or father of Donna was a little Morgan called Watchmaker. So it must have been a well-bred horse. Well, that is it. My father got right busy and he called my brother Richard, who was the oldest one. He graduated from Bowdoin the year I was born in 1907.[4]

"Well, so that was it. Pa got right busy and took one of the other horses and started out. They alerted people along the way as to what they were all up to. The pung had a different width runner because of its shape, so they could follow that track knowing what they were looking for. They followed the tracks to where they stopped in front of the barn. They went in and got the pitchforks, and it wasn't long before the prisoners got out of the hay-mow. They were sent to the state prison for five years. Nobody seems to know who they were, but that is it. That is quite a story, isn't it? It will get you going![5]

"The story of Donna reminds me of the farm.[6] You know, Pa was a farmer from the time he was born. He didn't want to be anything but a farmer, and Grampa could see it. After a while, he decided it was no use try-ing to make a businessman out of Pa. Grampa did send him to business school in Portland.[7] He did all the hon-orable things and gave him land here and there—think-ing he might speculate, I guess, but it was no use. All the time my father wanted to be a farmer, and he was a farmer and he loved it. I guess you might as well say that we all loved it, too.

"I think growing up on a farm did more than any-thing to make me who I am. If you think about it, now you have to get a book to teach a kid how the sex of this or that comes. When you lived on a farm, you knew that the sheep would deliver a baby lamb. You knew that the cat was going to have kittens. You knew that the rooster chased the hen and sat on her. You knew all those things without anybody telling you. I can't think of any place where you could get a better education without a book. You picked it up as you went along. Well, of course it was the happiest place I could have been, because I spent all my time in the barn with the lambs. Now here's a story for you.

Pa feeding his flock in the Dow pasture, summer 1920
COLLECTION OF MARY ANN AND JOHN VINTON

"We had sheep and we had pigs, and we had cows and we had everything. The lambs, of course, were mine. Especially when there were two, and the mother couldn't feed both of them. I always had the bottle lambs. I was over visiting my aunt in Damariscotta and my father came to pick me up and he said, 'We have a new lamb for you! One side of her face is white and one side is black.' They were Hampshire Downs, but this lamb was a mistake.

"I used to take her out and drive her around. I took her around town tied to a baby's sleigh. My sister Gladys had a very fancy one of those beautiful gold and white sleighs; they have a rollover on the front and velvet cushions and things. I used to tie her to that and drive her

Dorothy and Pa
COLLECTION OF MARY ANN AND JOHN VINTON

around the neighbors' downtown. All I did was use a piece of nice soft but firm rope and put it over her nose and around her head. That was Two Faces—that is what I named her, and that is what she went by. What do you think of that![8]

"Living on the farm was the best possible life. Everything about it was good. My father used to have hired men. They ate their dinner with us. My mother was a wonderful cook, and she always had good meals, especially during haying time, as it was hard work. Charles McKinney[9] was one of them. He took to me and treated me like a baby. They didn't have any children, and Ethel, his wife, was our schoolteacher. He took to me and called me Old Dorothy. He never called me anything but Old Dorothy.

Haying at Two Rivers Farm, Dyer's Neck
E. Joseph Leighton photograph, Ivan Flye Collection

"When he was out to get a load of hay and I was in the haymow, I would tramp the hay.[10] We would get back in and Charles would say, 'Now we have to get Old Dorothy off this load of hay.' He would hold out his arms and I would jump into them.

"Pa would always reward us for all our work. When the haying was over, we took a picnic to Pemaquid[11] and that was part of it, part of the life. I did everything with my father. He called me his boy. Here was Richard all grown up and away and there was me, and I followed that father of mine everywhere he went.

"In those days, everything had a season. We went blueberrying and blackberrying in the summer. There was one old man named Sargent who owned land up on the mountainside.[12] There were blueberries up there, and

Dorothy and friends in the Dow pasture, summer 1920
COLLECTION OF MARY ANN AND JOHN VINTON

he told my mother that we kids could go up there and he would show us where the blueberries were. So we would go up and pick two quarts. Going along with that, we had the Fairservice[13] family and all of them had a speech impediment. In those days kids were pretty busy and they could make some pocket money picking berries. Anyway, we had a doorbell and it would ring, and Doris would answer it, but there wouldn't be anybody there except a pail of blueberries. She'd look out and behind the maple tree in front of the house. This head would stick up and she would hear, 'Bewwies—ten cents.' So she would get her ten cents, and Bill Fairservice would come get his blueberry money. That is the way we lived. That was our life."

Dorothy settled back into her chair and paused a moment, eyeing me expectantly. I have had this experience before so rather than ask more questions, I waited. True to form, Dorothy shifted gears and pointed to a box full of small leather-bound diaries under her table and asked me to help her find one in particular. After a few minutes of searching I handed it to her, and she said, "Want to hear the story of the day I was born?" I nodded.

"You know, I don't exist anywhere except in Pa's diary.[14] Look here: It says under January 10, 1907, 'Pleasant and very cold morning. Baby girl born at 3 A.M. Flora doing fine.' That is the only place I am mentioned—not even in the town report. Lizzie, who was the midwife, told me all about the day I was born. She was eighty years old when she told me this story, as I had gone

Pa and Ma
COLLECTION OF MARY ANN AND JOHN VINTON

to see her in her nursing home before she died. We got to giggling and carrying on. It seems that my mother only wanted Liz for all her deliveries, and she had four. My father was married first and had three children, one boy and two girls. His first wife died of TB, and then my father got housekeepers until he met my mother and married her.

"Anyway, it was a cold, cold night, and the doctor had to come all the way from Damariscotta because I was coming feet first. Doctor King[15] must have come by horse. We had this big barn, and there was plenty of room to unhitch a horse and take him in and give him a load of hay so he would he comfortable. I was getting ready to come. You know there were no telephones or anything, so one of the neighbors had to go and fetch the doctor. My Aunt Dode was there, and she was a little high-strung.

"I was born in this old farmhouse where there was no regular heat. There was a stove in the kitchen, the usual stove, and next to it was the dining room. We didn't have any indoor plumbing or running water. This old house was pieces of other old houses that had been moved there and put together. The stove in the kitchen used the same chimney as the one in the dining room. Next to the kitchen was my mother's room, which is where she delivered me. Well, with this feet-first business, I took a long, long time a commin'. Lizzie was in the kitchen. They had to stay in the kitchen or the dining room to stay warm. When they brought me out, Lizzie was telling me, they brought me out to put me by the stove to warm up, and

Aunt Dode gave a shriek because I was so blue that I looked black. She was in a state! She didn't know what my mother had given birth to. How do you like that story? Can you imagine that happening today?

"When I think about childhood in Sheepscot, from my childhood and right up, it was a family affair to be a Sheepscot native when I was a kid. The families and the neighbors were like nursemaids; it was the life I was living that I was so happy about. It was the life, the beautiful life. We learned things we needed to know to go with that life. All these new inventions that they are using, I don't use any of them. Everything is gone. People think that they can come back to it but they never will. We are never going back and we are on our way. We can't stop to think. I have lived a life that is just like that. Now I am living someone else's life, and it is just like that. You see what I mean? It is funny, how you take it all around."

Dorothy is a practiced and experienced storyteller. As she talks, her face is animated, and she often takes on the voices of the characters in her stories. The young Fairservice child, for example, is forever speaking with a slight lisp. Aunt Dode carries on in a high-pitched voice, and the burglars slip into and out of the barn in a whisper. As she tells a story, Dorothy leans forward for the dramatic moments and then sits back, eyeing me to see if I am paying attention. Her voice lowers and her eyes narrow to convey mock anger, and she laughs often at the absurdity of the situation. She is totally engaging and totally engaged.

Her stories are tidy and well crafted. She weaves them from memory and bits of writing and artifacts from the past. The story of her birth is encapsulated in Pa's diary. As was the custom of the time, Pa made faithful daily entries in a little leather book that would fit in his shirt pocket. Each page was divided into days, and a whole week was laid out on pages facing each other. Each day had only room for a sentence or two. The ability to summarize even the most complicated of events in a few words is an art form that may have belonged to another time.

"The Whole Family, 1907." Front row: Ruth, Alice, Gladys.
Back row: Marion, Richard, Doris holding baby Dorothy.
COLLECTION OF MARY ANN AND JOHN VINTON

It is easy to return to the two lines in her father's diary and think again about the power of narrative to flesh out the events of history. Without Dorothy's tale of stoves and birthing on a hard winter's night, we would be left without any insight into what life on a Maine farm was really like. The facts surrounding her birth were potentially gruesome, and the consequences might have been grave.[16] The line, "Flora doing fine" means much more now in the context of the story. I imagine that Pa had some anxious moments, along with the doctor from Damariscotta, and that Aunt Dode's outburst was comic relief.

At one point in our conversation, Dorothy asks me to hand her a photo album. The cover is heavy gray cardboard, and the spine is tied together with black ribbon. It is faded from the sun and years of handling. Each of the dark pages reveals a few black and white photographs, their edges held in place by satin album corners glued carefully to the pages. Underneath each photograph is a title and a date, neatly lettered in the kind of white ink that was readily available at the local five-and-dime. Dorothy holds the album in her lap, staring down at each picture and telling me who it is and what event it recalls. She turns the pages slowly, as if walking backward through her life and times.

The photos date from the early part of the century to just after World War I. The people stare out of the pictures, captured in various activities. There are shots of a young man in uniform on a station platform with his arm around a smiling woman holding a kitten. "That's Doris and Snookums," Dorothy says. "Doris came back from Nebraska in the summers, and one time she took home a kitten from the farm. She met her husband here, and they moved to Funk, Nebraska.[17] He died of TB." There are pictures of picnics, family gatherings, and the now-famous Grampa Carney's ninetieth birthday party. Her photo album has a picture of "Two Faces" and Pa Carney with a young heifer on a lead.

There is even a picture of Donna and a newspaper article about her from the *Lewiston Journal*'s illustrated magazine section of September 8, 1917. The headline reads, "Donna a Smart Horse at Thirty-four Years." Dorothy shows me the article and elaborates on the virtues of this amazing animal. The thieves are identified as James Monroe and John Freeman; they spent five years in prison for their efforts. To look at Sheepscot now, it is hard to imagine an event like this taking place. The back road to Damariscotta Mills is no longer a through street and the road into Damariscotta is Route 1. The bridge over Mill Creek was taken out years ago and the land is posted. It is no longer possible to take a shortcut from village to village, over back roads and paths that children could follow to school (Lincoln Academy) and piano lessons from the likes of Mrs. Viola True, who was listed in the *Maine Register*. Haggett's General Store burned down many years ago, and the idea of a search party armed with pitchforks to capture a pair of thieves is sweet and unthinkable. Yet at some level, events such as these tug at us and allude to a time that seems safer and more orderly, if only in our imaginations. Perhaps this is the Maine that the freeway signs refer to as "The Way Life Should Be." For Dorothy, it is the way life was.

These pictures represent the bedrock of Dorothy's life—signposts showing the way to her farm, her parents, her family, and the village. As I listen to her talk, it is like being in a time machine; the destination is a place in the past that I would never know without her. Clearly these early years for Dorothy were happy ones, as life on Echo Farm, at least from a child's point of view, was idyllic.

At one point in our conversation about the farm, Dorothy stops talking and eases back into her chair. She looks suddenly small and frail, as if the weight of years and memory are almost too much for her. I, too, am quiet. In my mind's eye, I wander back to Sheepscot and to Echo Farm, finding it odd that long before I knew Dorothy and the history of the place, it was a house that I always liked. It is a spectacular piece of property that borders the "back" of the Sheepscot River. The new owners have done a good job restoring it. I wonder how they were able to do so without knowing its heart—what it once was, who lived there, and the stories that swirl around it.

Dorothy leans over and rummages around in the drawer next to her chair to find a picture of the farm. "See," she says, "here is the barn, and the sheep pen is in that corner. The tie-up is over on the other side, and there is the door to the stable where we used to drive the horses in. There was a mill in Sheepscot there on the falls,[18] and I guess you could buy cheap timber." The photograph is old and well worn, and yet Dorothy conjures up architectural details and miscellaneous vignettes without a moment's hesitation. "You know, it was only known as Echo Farm after my sister read a book about an Echo Farm. She liked it so much that she asked Pa if we could call our farm Echo Farm, after the one in the story. He said that would be fine by him, and from that day on, it was known as Echo Farm. The name has nothing to do with the place at all."

I tried to imagine what Echo Farm must have looked like with a barn full of hay and a busy family tending chores and putting food by. A farm is a very different place when the barns are full of animals and the land is tilled for crops than when it is no longer a working farm, and all of those activities fall silent. The change is significant, as it represents a shift in the use and value of land from a source of food and work to one of leisure, play, and speculation. For people like Dorothy, small working farms represent a way of life that extends to a worldview. Practicality, orderliness, and a combination of common sense, hard work, and good timing make the difference between a successful farm and a failure. When Dorothy was young, there were 48,000 of these farms in Maine; now there are less than 7,000. Most were handed down from generation to generation, providing a stable livelihood every bit as good as fishing and shipbuilding.[19] More important, they relied on a system of neighbors helping neighbors to make them run. Work and play at that time were one and the same thing.

I find it astounding that the only place where Sheepscot exists, as Dorothy knows it, is in her memory. The entire fabric of the village, the surrounding area, and even the state as a whole has changed so dramatically that, from Dorothy's perspective, it is virtually unrecognizable. Hence, for her, these stories are more than a way to entertain an appreciative stranger; they are a way to hold onto a place, a philosophy, and a way of life. They are the links that connect her to her family, her family to the village and farm, and the village and farm to the rest of the world. As I listen to Dorothy, I am once again struck by the degree to which the concept of "place" relies on the capacity of the human mind for its survival.

Sheepscot Village, looking south from Dyer's Neck, circa 1900
IVAN FLYE COLLECTION

As the afternoon wears on, Dorothy grows tired. I begin to pack up my recording gear, and we make another date to visit. She stops talking for a moment and looks out the window. The afternoon is fading as the buttery October light turns the river and the birches along its banks to gold. Like a true farmer, Dorothy comments, "It will be a full moon in a day or two, and if we get by without a hard frost, we might have another few days of warm weather." As I say good-bye and head for the door, she says to no one in particular, "So many stories." She shakes her head and murmurs again, "So many stories."

1 Newsletter of the Wiscasset-Waterville-Farmington Railway Museum, Sheepscot Station, Alna, Maine, Nov./Dec. 1999. The "narrow-gauge" refers to the railroad that ran from Wiscasset to Farmington, stopping in the little villages along the way. It was used to take children to school and to haul parcels and packages; it was also described as "accident-prone" because it derailed from time to time. Recently part of the little railroad has been resurrected by train enthusiasts complete with a web site: www.wwfry.org

2 Dorothy Carney Chase private collection: photographs.

3 George Dow, *Lincoln County News,* March 14, 2002, p. 9b. James Wilder Haggett operated a large general store and gristmill between 1889 and 1904. The store burned in 1904 but was rebuilt by John Coombs. It was located in Damariscotta Mills and was one of the stopping points for the thieves in Dorothy's story.

4 1906 United States Census. Dorothy's father had two wives; the first one died of tuberculosis. In the *Portland City Directory, 1875,* the number of cases of death by consumption was 188. Franklin then married Flora Sprague and had four more children: Gladys, Ruth, Alice, and Dorothy, the youngest. Richard and his sister Doris were from his first marriage.

Richard Carney graduated from Bowdoin in 1907, and his expenses for his final year in college were $347.00. Tuition at the time was $75.00, room was $54.00, and board was $140.00. His books came to about $11.00. Richard Carney graduated with 31 other young men, as Bowdoin was an all-male college until

1971. After graduation, he taught school for one year and then settled into a position as a chemical researcher for the Carnegie Institute in Boston. He died May 1, 1958, in Melrose, Massachusetts.

5 Doris Carney, "Donna a Smart Horse at Thirty-four Years," *Lewiston Journal,* Illustrated Magazine Section, Sept. 8, 1917. Among the inhabitants of Sheepscot, Donna is practically legendary. Pictures of the horse abound in Dorothy Carney Chase's private photograph collection. In the last eighty-nine years, at least two articles have appeared in the local paper, most recently in 1979. The articles include photos of the horse and a mention of how clever she is, because she holds up her foot to beg for food and snuffles in the pockets of smokers, looking for tobacco. The Donna story is also part of the storytelling repertoire of the Carney family and will be appearing in 2006 as a children's book, published by the Vermont Folklife Center in Middlebury, Vermont.

6 Echo Farm is located on the Sheepscot Road.

7 *Portland City Directory, 1875.* Levi Gray was the principal of Portland Commercial College, later known as "Gray's." In all probability, this was the business school that Franklin Carney attended.

8 Dorothy talked about a picture of the famous Two Faces, who indeed had a face that was half white and half black—apparently a mixture of Hampshire Downs and Dorset—but this photo didn't turn up later in her collection. Sheep farming was common in Maine in the early twentieth century. Sheep adapted easily to the Maine climate and provided wool and mutton.

9 *Annual Report of the Municipal Officers of the Town of Newcastle for the Year Ending 1909.* Charles McKinney and his wife, Ethel, were longtime residents of Sheepscot. Ethel was the schoolteacher as Dorothy was growing up. She was paid the huge sum of $9.00 a week for the fall, winter, and spring terms. Her school had an average of fifteen children in attendance.

10 Eric Sloane, *An Age of Barns* (New York: Funk & Wagnalls, 1967). The barn at Echo Farm is a classic example of "continuous architecture," which is unique to New England. Instead of the barns and outbuildings being separate structures, the weather dictated stringing the buildings together and attaching them to the main house, so that the farmer could do a whole day's worth of chores without going outside in bad weather. The way the buildings were linked varied from one part of New England to another. In Maine, as reflected in Dorothy's homestead, the house was connected to the barn via a summer kitchen and a utility/wood shed. On the other side of the barn and connected to it were smaller sheds. The barns opened in the front to the road and in the back to the pastures, thus eliminating the need to

drive livestock through traffic. The heart of the barn was the threshing floor, and the haymows existed on either side. Each mow had an access ladder. The hay was pitched by hand from the wagons into the mow, and children often had the job of "tramping" it down in order to be able to reduce the fluffiness and pack more hay into the mow. Livestock were fed by dropping the hay through open bays or pitching it into the feeding stations.

11 Fannie Hardy Eckstorm, *Indian Place-names of the Penobscot Valley and the Maine Coast*, Maine Studies No. 55 (Orono, Maine: University of Maine, 1974). "Pemaquid" refers to Pemaquid Harbor and Pemaquid Point, which was one of the first places in Maine that Europeans came ashore. John Smith arrived in 1614 and was followed by many others. The name "Pemaquid" is one of the few that have remained constant along the Maine Coast. It appears to have come from the Micmac and is one of the oldest words in their language. Regardless, it is a rugged piece of coastline where there is virtually no shelter from the sea.

At the time of Dorothy's childhood, Pemaquid was a small fishing community dominated by a lighthouse and Fort William Henry, which is an imposing stone structure at the entrance of Pemaquid Harbor. The Pemaquid Point Lighthouse is now the most photographed lighthouse in America and is surrounded by a state park. For an early history of Pemaquid, see Arlita Parker, *A History of Pemaquid* (Boston: McDonald and Evans, 1925).

12 Ava Chadbourne, *Maine Place Names and The Peopling of Its Towns* (Freeport, Maine: Bond Wheelwright Company, 1957), p. 4. The mountainside referred to is probably Job's Mountain in Alna, which was also the scene of neighborhood Fourth of July picnics.

13 "As a Veteran Saw It: Letter Written by Thomas Fairservice," June 18, 1843, printed in the *Boston Globe,* June 18, 1900. The letter, addressed to "Dear Sarah," recounts Thomas Fairservice's adventures in the dedication of the Bunker Hill Monument. He began his journey on the road from Wiscasset to Alna and walked to the village, where he hitched a ride with a friend and then took a steamer to Boston. It appears that Mr. Fairservice was a veteran of the Revolutionary War. He ends his letter as follows: "It is published in the papers that the records of the Revolutionary soldiers will soon be transmitted from Washington to this state. I shall take the opportunity to investigate as to any pension that I may be entitled to, I have seen more than I shall ever see again in this beautiful town of my nativity. Do excuse my writing as I write with a pen as bad as my writing is. I shall do all I can while here for the last time. Wishing you health and happiness, I remain yours, Thomas Fairservice."

14 Dorothy Carney Chase private collection: Franklin Irving Carney diaries. Franklin Carney kept a log of his activities in a small daily leatherbound diary. The entries dealt largely with weather conditions and farming activities. The diaries span a period of over forty years and, taken as a whole, give a laconic overview of farm life in the early twentieth century.

15 *Maine Register, State Year-book and Legislative Manual, no, 38, 1907–08* (Portland, Maine: Grenville M. Donham, 1907), p. 638, refers to a Dr. King of Damariscotta. Given the proximity of Sheepscot Village to Damariscotta and specifically the farmhouse, it is quite likely that Dr. King came from Damariscotta rather than the more famous but at the time elderly Dr. Card from Head Tide.

16 Theodore Caplow, et. al., *The First Measured Century: An Illustrated Guide to Trends in America 1900–2000* (New York: AEI Press, 2001), p. 26.

17 Nebraska State Historical Society marker 323. Funk, Nebraska, was named after Civil War veteran P. C. Funk, who came to Phelps County in 1877 and bought 160 acres of land. The town thrived due to access made possible by the Colorado Railroad Line between Axtell and Holdrege. The first grain elevator was built there by L. T. Brookings, who also became the editor of the *Funk Enterprise,* the town newspaper. The town survived three serious fires as well as the hardship of the depression years. Irrigation brought water to the area in 1938, which improved life for the townspeople and farmers.

 The current population of Funk is 198, and visitors to the town can participate in the Phelps County Fair in July, in crane watching in March–April, or in Swedish Days in the summer. There is one bed-and-breakfast that accommodates visitors to Funk.

18 Paul Rivard, *Maine Sawmills: A History* (Augusta, Maine: Maine State Museum, 1990). This volume contains photos and explanations of the various types of sawmills in Maine, including the portable sawmills mentioned in Dorothy's story.

19. U.S. Department of Commerce, *Historical Statistics of the United States* (Washington, D.C.: Bureau of the Census, 1975).

A Sheepscot parade coming off the bridge
E. JOSEPH LEIGHTON COLLECTION, LINCOLN COUNTY HISTORICAL ASSOCIATION

Chapter Four

EVERYONE KNEW YOU
Childhood in the Village

I arrive for this visit having read and listened to much of Dorothy's stories from previous sessions. The village is beginning to take on a life of its own and I ask her about it. "What was it like to grow up in Sheepscot back then?" She doesn't hesitate, just nods her head as if she has anticipated my question and begins.

"It was a family affair to be a Sheepscot native when I was growing up. Take Louise, for example. Louise Marsh[1] was my playmate. She was born in September [of 1906] and I was born in January. When we were old enough to go to school, which was four, I think, she and I were just like this." Dorothy holds up her hand with her fingers crossed. "Louise's mother had nine kids, and my mother just had me at home.... I was the last one, so I was kind of loose. My three sisters were up in the square schoolhouse on the hill.

"I used to get lonesome, so I would tease my mother to go down and visit. My mother had an understanding with Iva Marsh[2] that if she didn't want me, she was to send me home. Mother used to tell me, 'You go and tell Iva that you can stay two minutes.' And I used to go down to that door and I'd say, 'Momma said I could stay two minutes.' She'd say, 'Okay,' and that is the last time you would hear from Iva until it was time to go home for dinner. Anyway, that was Louise, and she and I hung out together. She had to look out for the next one down, Herbert, who was a holy terror.[3]

"You know he almost burned the school down. Our school never had more than one room.[4] We faced down to the teacher's desk. The boys had a dressing room and the girls had a dressing room. We had an outhouse in the back and a woodshed to the north. Cliff Marsh was the janitor for a long time, and he would bring a pail of water from the spring each morning into the schoolroom, and there was a dipper. We all drank out of the dipper.

"We had a big wood stove for heat. Cliff Marsh would make a fire in the stove every morning and keep it going through the dinner hour and during the day. We all went home to dinner at twelve. Everyone in Sheepscot ate dinner from twelve to one and had supper at night. Anyway, they sent the little kids home first. Well, Cliff had a fire poker that he used to stir up the stove. It had a wooden handle and for some reason, he left it in the stove too long, so the handle caught on fire.

"Yessuh, well, Cliff goes to the front door, the only door, and throws it out into the snow bank. It was winter, so there was snow on the ground outside. That was the smart place to put it until he could fix it. The primary kids got sent home a little ahead of the rest of us, and that meant that Herbert had already left. Not too

Garrison Hill School, Sheepscot, 1910.
Dorothy is second from left in the front row.
COLLECTION OF MARY ANN AND JOHN VINTON

long later, we started to go home. Well, Cliff began looking for his fire poker and he couldn't find it anywhere.

"Herbert had found it and took the burning end of the stick and stuck it up under the clapboards on the north side of the schoolhouse. Cliff had to get right busy and get an ax and chop the clapboards out to get the fire out and not burn down the whole building." Dorothy laughs uproariously.

"Here is another story about Herbert. Oh, God, he was a terror. There were apple trees all around Sheepscot and the school. But there was this very old apple tree, you can just visualize how hollow it was and how all these openings came up on it. It was all bark inside and dry. Well, Herbert got a fire going in that. It was hilarious, really, because all those little holes had smoke coming out of them. It was a sight!

"It was my father's property, and the schoolteacher was scared to death. Of course, it would be dangerous if the wind came up in the night; it could have burned up everything in the town.[5] So one of the kids was sent down to get my father, who was right there on the doorstep. Mother said he came home and just doubled up with laughter. He said it was the funniest thing he'd ever seen, but he had to go up and be very serious about all this. He had to speak sharply to Herbert and the other kids.

"Oh, I have so many stories that go with everything. Here's another one. There was a family that lived in Sheepscot named Pottle.[6] They had lots of kids and lived out on a farm on the back road. They didn't have a lot, but they made do with most everything. The kids all came to school with the rest of us. When the youngest came, his name was Albert; the teacher gave him a seat in the back of the room with the other little kids. He was afraid of people and cried all day until he could sit with his sisters and brothers up front.

"Anyway, Herbert, who was always full of mischief, asked to go to the bathroom. He was excused and went out to the outhouse. Well, he never returned. He was known for setting fire to the school and to the apple tree and things, so there was cause for concern. The teacher waited and waited, but no Herbert, so she sent Albert out to see what happened to him. Well, Albert didn't come back, either. Time went by and time went by until, finally, Albert and Herbert came back together. It seems that Herbert had lost the only button on his pants and they were falling down, so he couldn't come back into the schoolroom. Albert, because he lived in the woods and knew how to do everything with nothing, found a twig and made Herbert a new button for his pants. Now isn't that a cute story?

"Oh, yes, there are lots of stories that go with us growing up in Sheepscot in those early years.... I have some good stories about the narrow-gauge. The narrow-gauge went back and forth to Wiscasset and to other places. That is how I got to school later on—which is another story—but this one is about my husband Ross and his pal Harold when they were kids.

"There was a brook where they could go trout fishing

back of the narrow-gauge. They got out there, and the section men were riding and fixing the rails. You know how those old section cars work, don't you? They had handles that pumped up and down to make the car move. You stood on a platform with a pillar in the middle.[7] Well, Harold and Ross got out there, and the section men had gone around the corner. It was dinnertime, I guess. Anyway, it was just too much of a temptation.

"These two kids got on the section car and started it going—only it got going so fast that they couldn't stop it. It raced right down the tracks when up ahead they saw the flat car which had a bumper on the end where the men were sitting and eating lunch. It was blueberry time, and they had their lunch pails full of blueberries. Well, Ross and Harold crashed into that car, and all the lunch boxes with blueberries went flying. Ross and his pal were scared and ran off into the bushes. The section men didn't even look for them. I guess they were used to it.

"You know, I was on the narrow-gauge when it got derailed.[8] Yessuh! Now here's a story for you.

"I went to primary school in Sheepscot, and after that, I went to Hebron Academy. Education was always important to my family, so we got sent to school. My sisters went to Kent's Hill, but I went to Hebron. Anyway, I always came home on the train. It would be vacation time, and it was spring, when all the frost was coming out of the ground and the roads were usually terrible, as they were dirt. My father had one horse injured from stepping in a frost hole, and it couldn't work anymore. So he was thinking that I was going back to school, which would be around March or April, I must have been about thirteen at the time, and there was nothing on the roads around then but mud—just nothing. Pa decided he would put me on the narrow-gauge and save himself a trip on those bad roads and the chance of having another horse fall in a hole. So he took me out and left me for the train. I got on and it wasn't more than half a mile when it went off the track entirely.

"I had my watch on—they said it was lucky to have a watch when you were that young. I think I earned it somewhere. Anyway, Cliff Marsh was on that train and of course I was talking to him. I said it was no use, Pa couldn't come get me on account of the roads, and there wasn't another train up from Sheepscot before four in the afternoon. So I said to Cliff that I was going to walk home. It was Monday, so my mother was doing the wash in the kitchen when I opened the door. She thought I had gone to school. She just looked up and didn't say a word. I said, 'I forgot my toothbrush.'

"Now that is the story from the narrow-gauge."

I can tell from Dorothy's expression that there are more stories to come. She is brimming with them as she dashes pell-mell into a time and place that feels eons, not just decades, removed from this particular afternoon in her assisted-living facility. Dorothy's mother is a prime example of Yankee composure; she manages to maintain an extraordinary degree of calm as her beloved daughter walks unexpectedly in the door—home from a train

The narrow-gauge at Sheepscot Station

E. JOSEPH LEIGHTON COLLECTION, LINCOLN COUNTY HISTORICAL ASSOCIATION

wreck. Dorothy shifts gears and suddenly the narrow-gauge is left behind and the scows of the river come to the forefront.

"We also had scows that went up and down the river.... We kids used to like the scows. Captain Joe Jones[9] ran up and down the Sheepscot and back and forth to Portland carrying cargo to and from the villages. For example, we heated our house with coal, and Captain Jones used to haul the coal up the river, and Pa would go down with a horse and wagon and pick it up. That was the only way to get it there. If you wanted anything of any size to it, such as a piece of furniture, it had to come up the river on the scows.[10]

"Anyway, he [Captain Jones] had two scows, one the *North Star* and the other the *Yankee,* and he had a motor boat to run them. We used to hear the whistle blow when he was coming up the river. No matter where we kids were, we would all rush down to the bridge, because they had to open the draw. He [Captain Jones] had to wait to go through because he had a mast. The bridge was on a track and always came apart, so we all liked to see what was going on. We had to be down there to see the draw open and the ship come through.

"In the wintertime, there wasn't anything going down the Sheepscot, because it was frozen up. Captain Jones pulled the scows up on Chase's Point to store them for the winter.[11] His daughter, Josephine, was a pal of my sister Alice. They went down and had their lunch on the scows, as if they were going to sea. My mother made Alice watch me, and I would take Louise, so we got to go on these picnics.

"As I started to tell you about Louise," Dorothy said, finally circling back to the beginning of our conversation, "I think you would think it was interesting about two kids of nine or ten. It was unusual for girls then to do what we did.

"I was allowed to use my father's tools, his hammer and saws and things. My father never said a word. So Louise and I—this was Sheepscot back in those early days—took my father's hod with the brightest nails, we had a hammer (remind me about the hammer—there is a story there) and a saw. I don't think we had an ax, because I wasn't allowed an ax. So we went up and we decided to build ourselves a playhouse. Yessuh!

"We were nine or ten years old, and we built ourselves a playhouse. There was a tree, probably a cherry tree, and it grew in two forks. There were posts left over from the fence. All the fences in Sheepscot were wood in those days, from the lumber mills up the river. The tree made a triangle, and we worked from there. I think we put a window in it. We had a door on the north side, and some of it was on a slope, so you had to put your head down to get in.

"Can you imagine? We thought it was a pretty nice playhouse, and I don't think we went there except for once or twice. Building it was the satisfaction. I can't remember where we got it—I think it was a piece of an old harness—but we had a door that had leather hinges.

Captain Walter Jones's scow at Dyer River bridge
E. JOSEPH LEIGHTON COLLECTION, LINCOLN COUNTY HISTORICAL ASSOCIATION

Why I wanted to tell you about the hammer is this. My father told me years and years later when I was visiting him just before he died, 'You know, Dorothy, some of the boys went out there and tore down the playhouse. They brought me back my favorite hammer that I hadn't been able to find for a long, long time.' You know, he laughed!"

I asked Dorothy what became of all these people from her childhood.

"Well, Herbert went off to fight in the Pacific during World War II, and when he came back, he lived at home for a long time and never married. I don't think the war improved him any. I married Ross, but that was much later. He was thirteen years older than me and growing up, he was my hero. One of the other boys disappeared one night and was never seen again. Some say he fell off the bridge and drowned, but they never found a body. Others say something terrible happened to him; some even thought he had been murdered. His family contacted a psychic, but that didn't do any good. At any rate, he was never found.

"Louise—well, Louise became somebody. She went down to Portland to get a job. She ended up working at a hardware store. She was the kind that could keep on going until she was really more or less important. Margaret Chase Smith came along, you know, the senator from Maine, and Louise, in this hardware store, had a chance to meet and talk with her. Margaret needed some Maine people with her. So she gave Louise a job, and she worked with Margaret Chase Smith down in Washington, D.C. Then she came back and became head of one of the women's clubs in Portland. Louise became quite a person."[12]

The adventures of Dorothy and her friends read like an excerpt from *Tom Sawyer*. The cast of characters, a ragtag band of children, includes clever girls and mischievous boys, some with less than stellar reputations and a seemingly endless supply of adventures. Even the setting is similar. For Dorothy and her friends, the Sheepscot River is every bit as engaging and full of possibilities as the Mississippi. The only ingredient that seems to be missing is a villain. At least in this set of stories, no real harm comes to these children as they are growing up.

Just as in *Tom Sawyer*, the children of Sheepscot are generally left to do as they please, but within the boundaries of a shared community vision of acceptable behavior. Much of what goes on requires the unintentional if not overt complicity of the adults who work and live there. And, of course, it helps that these adults work either at home or very close by. Pa is available at a moment's notice to put out the fire in the apple tree. Mother is home doing the wash when Dorothy returns from the train derailment. It is particularly noteworthy that Mother doesn't have a great deal to say at this point. She simply looks up from her washing and, I imagine, questions Dorothy with a raised eyebrow.

The community provides a safety net that in turn promotes an easiness of movement and accessibility for these children that belies some of the physical risks these children take—risks that we find inconceivable. The definition of safety from Dorothy's perspective has more to do with social order than it has to do with physical danger.

There are other stories about boys leaping on the floating logs near the sawmill. The logs were poled down from the lumber lots upstream and bunched together in the millpond, a kind of holding tank. The logs provided an opportunity for "daring and bravery" amongst the young that is described this way by one of the participants: "On Saturdays and after school, these rolling logs were a rendezvous point. It was difficult to keep one's

Schooners at Bath Box, Sheepscot Reversing Falls, circa 1900
E. JOSEPH LEIGHTON PHOTOGRAPH, IVAN FLYE COLLECTION

balance as we skipped to and fro across them, and the inevitable usually happened as one went overboard into the water amidst the roars of laughter from your temporarily perpendicular mates."[13]

The narrow-gauge railroad, the subject of many adventures, looms large in the mythology of Sheepscot. The narrow-gauge, as it is affectionately called, served fourteen towns and ran from Wiscasset north and east. It was notorious for making unscheduled stops to pick up milk cans, produce, or the passengers who, like Dorothy, waited along the tracks and signaled the engineer when the train showed up. In its heyday, which was the early part of the century, the narrow-gauge transported 200,000 bushels of potatoes; had ninety-two freight cars, one baggage car, and four passenger cars; and employed more than eighty people.[14]

With a little research, I discovered that Ross and Harold were not the only two boys to lay claim to a free ride on the railroad. In fact, it seemed to be quite a common occurrence. Lawrence Averill, a childhood friend of Dorothy's, describes his adventures on the narrow-gauge in an unpublished memoir. He writes, "The engine was a boy's paradise. Living but a hop-skip-and-jump east of the depot, I used all the known wiles to ingratiate myself into the good favors of the engineer and the fireman, so successfully that I was borne in the cab of the 8:45 'down' trip to Wiscasset, returning on the 10:30 'up' train to Sheepscot. During the two-hour stop in Wiscasset, I strolled along the short main street, ogling the front windows. If I had a tightly squeezed penny in hand, which I did once in a blue moon, I invested it in a long stick of candy that I sucked with animation on the 'up' trip. I never failed to pull the whistle-cord with equal animation as the train sped through the deep woods that lined the right of way."[15]

I asked Dorothy about the possibility of this really occurring and read her the excerpt. "Oh, yes, a lot of the kids did that, and we also rode on the scows. Lots of the boys used to jump off the bridge and onto the scow as she was coming by and get a ride a little way up the river." As an afterthought and a way of placing the person, she added, "Oh, I remember Lawrence, he grew up to write books and other things!"[16]

As I listened to these stories, it occurred to me that by contemporary standards, the children of Sheepscot had a laissez-faire upbringing under the amused and watchful eye of adults. Their education was the basic fare of the one-room schoolhouse, they participated in one grand adventure after another, and without much effort, this whole scene could be awash in the glow of bucolic romanticism. Yet such an interpretation would be most unfair to the residents of Sheepscot and to an accurate view of child rearing and community expectation.

A case in point is Herbert Marsh. Herbert is more than just a busy, imaginative little boy. He, Louise, and the others are part of a tapestry of people and events against which the life of Dorothy and her immediate family is played out. Their stories of growing up frame yet another picture of Sheepscot, one that relies heavily on long-established relationships as a way of being known and understood in the community. Herbert is part of the same family that dug up Grampa and is the younger brother of Dorothy's best friend, Louise. Dorothy and Louise are generally responsible for Herbert's well-being, regardless of his propensity for getting himself into mischief. He is described as happy and laughing, and one can surmise from the inventiveness of his antics that he is bright. Despite the fact that he could have burned down the school and, without too much effort, the entire town, there is no mention of severe punishment for this boy. He is not being referred to the school psychologist, nor is his mother seeking medical intervention from the family pediatrician. Rather, Iva Marsh has her hands full with other children and other events, and the community provides a benevolent safety net.

The raising of Herbert, as was the case with most children of the day living in small coastal villages, resides not only with the family but also with the community at large. The community's protective oversight depends, in turn, on relationships that span generations and are anchored in a stable view of place that, paradoxically, offers young people great freedom. Whatever growing up in Sheepscot may lack in terms of adult supervision,

Sheepscot Village, looking east from Dyer's Neck
E. JOSEPH LEIGHTON COLLECTION, LINCOLN COUNTY HISTORICAL ASSOCIATION

it fosters great personal responsibility on the part of the child.

The children's access to the train and the scow—dangerous play by today's standards—is considered not only acceptable behavior but part of their preparation for work and adulthood. Their adventures on the railroad, in the mill yard, and on the scows provide them with a kind of apprenticeship. As they experience rolling logs or sitting next to the engineer, they are immersed in a tutorial that invites them into these occupations. The working adults give tips and mini-lessons, and in some cases, the child's play becomes the adult's livelihood. For example, it is entirely possible that Captain Jones, the father of two daughters, found an able and interested listener in one of

Friends on the houseboat at the Sheepscot bridge.
Dorothy is on the right.
COLLECTION OF MARY ANN AND JOHN VINTON

the children leaping off the bridge onto his boat—a boy who, with the proper training, could take over the business someday. Young people became members of the working community early on, and these adventures allowed them to enter the adult world in a seamless fashion.

Even the story of Dorothy's playhouse is instructive. Tools were more valuable in those days, because they were expensive and hard to replace. And yet Dorothy's father was more than willing to let the two girls take his favorite hammer and a hod of shiny nails out to the "back forty."

Ice cream stand at a Sheepscot celebration.
Flora Sprague Carney with a baby carriage is at far left.
E. JOSEPH LEIGHTON COLLECTION, LINCOLN COUNTY HISTORICAL ASSOCIATION

As Dorothy explains, it wasn't building a finished playhouse that was important; it was the freedom to build it and the satisfaction of having done so. She and Louise barely spent any time there after it was finished. The process of construction and decision-making, as well as the lack of adult direction and supervision, gave the girls a taste of independence, an opportunity to do the kind of work that was generally reserved for boys, and an outlet for their creativity and problem-solving skills.

The one-room schoolhouse has long been part of the New England educational tradition, and Sheepscot is no exception. The early establishment of these schools came with built-in expectations for students' behavior. In a letter of instruction to an unknown teacher, the town secretary writes, "We require of all scholars good morals and submissive orderly behavior, and we request you to inform us of immorality in conduct, disobedience to orders, and disrespectful behavior either in or out of school, that such offenders may be removed and their places filled with persons more deserving."[17] Harsh words with little room for interpretation.

One-room schools provided a unique form of instruction that relied on a locally known teacher (usually a woman), small numbers of children, and a heavy dose of student interaction and peer tutoring. It was probably the latter two that allowed children to move along at their own pace and with a remarkable degree of success. This model of multi-age education in the early twentieth century gave students a solid grounding in the basics of lit-

Looking across the Sheepscot bridge;
the Dyer River bridge is on the left.
E. Joseph Leighton Collection, Lincoln County Historical Association

eracy, numeracy, civics, and geography. Dorothy's peers all learned to read, write, and speak with a high degree of fluency. They were educated children who, despite their antics, grew up to be reasonably successful adults who took their places in the community and the world.

Louise Marsh is a prime example of how far one could go with a Sheepscot education. At a very early age, Louise changed her name to Teddy—the name by which she was known for the rest of her life and which appears on her tombstone. She donned pants as a young woman and became a social activist and reformer, much beloved by her family and her community. Her extensive letters to Senator Margaret Chase and to members of her family while she was in Washington underscore this point. They are full of news and reflect her concern with the current issues of the day, both in Maine and in the nation. They are articulate, informative, and insightful. Louise did indeed, as Dorothy suggests, "become somebody."

Concern about the quality of education was real, and I found bits and pieces of what constitutes good and bad teaching in the town report. Commenting on the failure of a young teacher, the superintendent writes, "Miss Winnifred Erskine of Alna commenced the spring term of the school but made some mistakes on account of youth and inexperience, and left at the end of two weeks." This implies that perhaps the students were more rowdy than Dorothy remembers. In any case, "youth and inexperience" are not among the reasons to fire a young teacher today. On a more positive note, "The fall term of this school [Sheepscot] was taught by Miss Ruth Bartlett of the Mills. Miss Bartlett is a wide-awake and faithful instructor and did good work in this respect. There was some disorderly conduct on the part of a few of the boys toward the close of the term. In such cases the teacher should at once send the offenders home, inform their parents and the Superintendent of the offense, and await action." The superintendent closes his remarks with the following: "And now retiring from office, I would express my thanks to the School Committee for their assistance; the parents for their cooperation; the teachers for their faithful work; and would assure the children, the most of whom I know by name, that I shall always remember them and pray for them with interest and affection, hoping they may all become noble men and women and accomplish much good in the world."[18]

I thought about the superintendent's prayer for the children of Sheepscot. We would wish nothing less for our own children to become noble and accomplish good in the world. Yet how hard it seems to make this happen. I wonder how much we have lost and gained in the last eighty years. I could not help but wonder if children today wouldn't benefit from village life and the close proximity of working adults rather than the cyberworld where many children spend so much time.

1 *Portland Press Herald*, September 3, 1993, p. 8B. "Louise "Teddy' Marsh, secretary for Maine Supreme Court," (obituary).

2 Staff Writer, *Face of Maine Portland Press Herald*, November 14, 1963 (retrieved from the archives of Senator Margaret Chase Smith). Iva Marsh was born in Jefferson, Maine, and came to Sheepscot in 1901, where she married Horace Marsh. She and her husband had nine children, all born at home, and lived "on the four corners." The four corners is an intersection in the middle of the village. She is described in the article at eighty-one as "always busy, often alone but not lonely. She reads and knits and keeps the home spic and span." In her later years, she wrote a column for the *Lincoln County News*. "I can write when the summer residents arrive, but not when they leave for the winter. They don't want it advertised their homes are shut up. I only write what happens this side of the bridge. A neighbor— you can see her house over there—reports the news on her side of the bridge. That's . the "T'other Side of Sheepscot news'." Considering the size of the village and the length of the bridge, it is hard to imagine that there was enough local news to warrant this geographic distinction. Iva Marsh, like Dorothy, embodies the values, interests, and independence of a generation of women in rural Maine.

3 Herbert Bragg Marsh, December 19, 1907–March 13, 1967. In actuality, Louise was fifteen months older than Dorothy, who was virtually the same age as Herbert. They were, in fact, born less than a month apart, yet Herbert was definitely relegated to "younger" status and became the charge of the two girls.

4 Dorothy Carney Chase private collection: photograph of the Sheepscot grammar school. The one-room schoolhouse in Sheepscot, where Dorothy's sister Doris at

one time presided as teacher, was a hip-roofed square building built in the 1800s. The children varied in age, and the number of students was dependent on the village population. Dorothy had approximately fourteen children in her class, ranging in age from five to fourteen. Dorothy's sister Ruth also taught in Sheepscot and appears in the *Report of the Superintendent of Schools for 1920.*

5 Fire was a very real concern in these little villages, where buildings were close together and the fire department—all volunteer—was often no match for high winds and tough weather conditions, especially in the winter. Sheepscot had had its share of fires, including one that burned the mill and the general store in October 1906. Herbert's prank could easily have had dire consequences.

6 The United States Census, 1900–30. The Pottle family appears in the US Census for Newcastle, Maine. Pottles are buried in the Alna cemetery as far back as 1839 (New England Historic Genealogical Society database). No mention, however, of an Albert Pottle exists in the vital records. Albert is probably a nickname or an error. It is clear from the Lincoln County Vital Records that there were several school-aged children with the last name of Pottle; all were close in age and would have attended the one-room schoolhouse at the same time as Dorothy. There is also evidence in the record of deeds that a Pottle family owned a farm in Sheepscot.

7 Ivan Flye Historical Photo Collection, Nobleboro Historical Society, # 474. This photo shows the section men on the infamous push carts that were so tempting to the boys of the surrounding towns.

8 Ivan Flye Historical Photo Collection, Nobleboro, # 604. The derailing of the narrow-gauge was a relatively common occurrence. This was usually more of an inconvenience than a danger. However, occasionally the narrow-gauge would suffer a major catastrophe and the engine would tip over. There were few injuries despite how it appeared.

9 Crowley Collection (obituaries, funeral notices), twentieth century, Wiscasset Public Library. "Joseph R. Jones. Occupation: capt retired coasting born in Alna January 11 1866 died July 25 1959 age 93 lived on the King's Highway in Sheepscot, Survived by two daughters, Josephine and Nina. Captain Jones was a direct descendent of Joseph Jones, who was a sea captain during the Revolutionary War."

10 Ava Chadborne, *Maine Place Names and the Peopling of its Towns* (Freeport, Maine: Bond Wheelwright, 1957). The scows carried cordwood, bailed hay, lumber, and other goods to the metropolitan markets. Captain Jones's vessels, the *North Star* and the *Yankee,* were among the last of the coasting scows to sail on the upper Sheepscot. An article in the Aug. 8, 1948, *Portland Sunday Telegram,* "Sleepy

Sheepscot," by Mark Hennessy describes the scow captains as "a hardy breed of river men who handled the flat-bottomed scows, running them regularly between Alna and the downriver villages." Ivan Flye Historical Photo Collection, Nobleboro Historical Society, #1341, shows a picture of the scow *North Star*.

11 Ivan Flye Historical Photo Collection, Nobleboro Historical Society, #1340.

12 Margaret Chase Smith Library, archives of correspondence between Senator Chase and Louise Marsh, including photocopies of newspaper clippings and letters to the editor written by Louise Marsh in support of Senator Chase. *Portland Sunday Telegram*, February 17, 1963. "Louise T. Marsh was named assistant secretary on the staff of U.S. Senator Margaret Chase Smith. She had been a cashier at Edwards Walker & Co." Louise Marsh took the name Teddy very early on, and in fact signed all her correspondence to Senator Chase as "Affectionately, Teddy." She was active in politics from the middle 1960s until her death in 1993.

13 Lawrence Averill, *Sheepscot Story: Chronicles of a Maine Village in Three and a Half Centuries* (unpublished ms.), Maine Historical Society, p. 20.

14 Ibid., p. 21.

15 Ibid., pp. 22–23.

16 Nancy Burncoat's letter, *Sunday Telegram* (Worcester, Massachusetts), March 29, 1942. This letter is a brief sketch of the summer life of the "writing Averills," as Lawrence and his wife were known. Dr. Averill taught psychology at a teachers' college, but their real love seems to have been "Ancestral Acres," the home place of Lawrence in Sheepscot. They restored the house and spent their mornings writing and their afternoons making calls and doing housework, etc. As quoted in the article, "Toward sunset, each one stops whatever it is they may be doing and converges on the landing and the picturesque shoreline, where the gulls are screaming. There they put aboard a picnic supper and with any friends who may be available at the moment eat out in the harbor and come home by moonlight if any, starlight if not." This bucolic existence is complete with a visit to local artists, addresses to Senator Smith, and various civic activities. Their book, *Pie for Breakfast*, published in 1957, gives an account of their first year of retirement in Sheepscot and offers an interesting glimpse into life in rural Maine in the early 1940s.

17 Letter to teacher, Miscellaneous Box # 87, Wiscasset Public Library, Local History Collection.

18 "Report of the Superintendent of Schools," *Annual Report of Newcastle, 1909*, p. 59.

Sheepscot Village from the Golden Ridge
E. JOSEPH LEIGHTON COLLECTION, LINCOLN COUNTY HISTORICAL ASSOCIATION

Chapter Five

YOUR OX DIED
Social Relations

*W*e have to go beyond the kids, you know," Dorothy says eagerly as I walk in the door on what passes for an early spring day in Maine. The trip from North Carolina is a reminder of just how different the seasonal timetable is here: our daffodils and tulips are out, while Maine still has patches of snow. The days are brighter, however, and winter is on the wane. I have been traveling frequently for the last few weeks and sending Dorothy postcards, which she displays on the table next to her elbow. She is glad to see me and is in high humor, her eyes twinkling. There is no doubt that this is going to be an interesting session, and I can barely get my recording gear set up before she starts in.

"Don't you want to know about the other characters in the village? I have lots of stories for you there. There was always something going on. You may think that Sheepscot was this quiet little place. Nosuh! There was all sorts of belligerency. Here's a good one for you. I can tell you about the Flyes." Dorothy pauses momentarily to collect her thoughts and make sure I am paying attention. Then she begins.

"There were three brothers—Edwin, Harry, and Albion—and they fought like cats and dogs. Albion lived over on the North Newcastle Road, and he had the largest barn you would ever want to see, and in front of it was a darling little house. It had a sloping roof and a lovely little vestibule. The barn was huge. You know why? So his brother Harry, who lived across the way on Dyer's Neck,[1] couldn't see what he was doing in his backyard. That is the truth of the story that I've got. You don't know the half of it." She starts to chuckle. "Here's another one about the Flyes—they were somethin'."

"Edwin lived up next to Grampa,[2] and he didn't get along with him too well, either. Grampa used to try to buy the field in front of his house so the Flyes wouldn't get it and put something up there—Mother told me this. Whenever Harry would see his brother Edwin coming up the road, he would go right straight to his front porch. He would stand there and say in this big loud voice that you could hear for miles, 'There goes the man that killed Wash Houdlette.[3] There goes the man who stole my sheep.' There goes the man that did this or did that, whatever it was that was irritating to Harry at the time. I don't think it made much difference if it was true or not.

"The other brother, Albion, had a wife who never called him anything but Mr. Flye.[4] She didn't call him Albion, just Mr. Flye. They lived on a farm down on the other side and one noontime they were having dinner. Albion said to his wife, 'Well,' he said, 'this cow Molly is getting too old. I think I will have her butchered.'

"His wife said, 'Oh, Mr. Flye, I have always loved Molly and I hate to see it. Can't we just keep her?'

"It seems that this went on and on. One day they were having beef and he said, 'You enjoying your dinner, Mrs. Flye?' 'It is very nice, Mr. Flye,' she said. 'Ayuh,' he said, 'nice piece of old Molly!'"

At the end of this story, Dorothy breaks into gales of laughter and then barrels on.

"Well, it came time for Albion to get ready to die. Horace Marsh—you know, that same family—well, he was one of those that sat up at night with the old men when they were dying. They had a little liquor there on the table and Horace didn't mind imbibing now and again through the night as Old Albion kept on living. It was getting towards morning, and Albion died. They sent for the undertaker.[5] The undertaker came, but it was so near morning that he said he couldn't stay to prepare Albion because he had to get to a funeral he was running. But, he said, 'I have brought everything with me.' (They were going to put fluid in. I don't know how they do it, do you?) But Horace said, 'I know how to do that'— which isn't true. Horace did not know a thing about it, but he had been drinking, and the undertaker took him at his word and got him started and then went off and left him.

"Horace got drunker and drunker, and blew Albion up until he was quite huge. So Albion came out being bloated great big. Horace went and told Mrs. Flye that he had her husband all arranged and would she like to see him. She went into the parlor, and here was this blown-up man that had been her husband. The story is that she looked down on him and said, 'Conquered at last, Mr. Flye,'[6] and walked out.

"Here is another one. There was old Nat West, who lived over on the Alna side in a nice house. All those Wests were from down on the back road to Wiscasset. Nat West had that nice big house on the corner. The story that went with Nat, when I was young, is that he opened the barn doors—you know how they slide—which was right there on the main highway and sat down and shot himself. That was what happened to him. There was a lot of talk about all that. A lot of insanity and mental problems ran in that family. I remember my father washing his wagon and grumbling about it before he went to Nat West's funeral.

"You want a funny one?" I nod, but I know perfectly well that it doesn't make a bit of difference what I want. The story will be upon me before I know it.

"Well, across the street from the Wests' was the Sargent house, and there were two brothers, Henry and Manley Sargent, living in it. They did not get along too well. So they had two doorways and two sets of stairs, so they wouldn't have to see each other. My mother-in-law told me this one. She used to deliver milk down there when she was a kid. She went down, and Manley had come home with a wife, and the mother-in-law wasn't too happy about it, and she said she needed more milk for her 'guests'—meaning, of course, Manley's new wife.

*Sheepscot Village from Job's Mountain, Alna, looking east.
The Sargent house is at the intersection, in the center
foreground. A second entry door is visible on the left.*

E. JOSEPH LEIGHTON PHOTOGRAPH,
COLLECTION OF ALEXANDER AND KELLY PATTON BROOK

"Manley was quite a carpenter. It was said that he built a camp on his property that was so tight that when he went out there one night in a fit of rage and slammed the door, it blew out all the windows. Oh yes, he was quite the builder. He built a boat that wasn't to his satisfaction, so he chopped it up and built another one.[7]

"He and his brother were smart but strange men. Henry was very shy. He would only sing in church if he could go down to the furnace room and sing from there. Well, he made a big invention that had to do with the streetcars—it was like a horse-starter or something. He got a lot of money for it and bought a nice house in

Manley Sargent with his wife and step-daughter in front of his one-room structure
E. JOSEPH LEIGHTON PHOTOGRAPH, COLLECTION OF W. H. BUNTING

Boston. When he moved in, the story goes that he ripped out all the electrical wires because he said it 'warn't safe.' Yessuh, they were some peculiar.[8]

"Anyway, Lawrence Averill told me this one about Manley. Lawrence grew up to be a preacher,[9] so he would have told the truth. There was another school over in Alna—they all looked alike, they were square and had one room. This one was up on the bank on the opposite side of the Sargents' home. It was a hot day, and they had a lot of windows open. Lawrence and his friend Luther Carney were sitting in the back seats of the schoolhouse, because those were the seats reserved for the bigger boys. He said that Manley always liked to soak his feet in the salt water, but he had to wait for high tide to take his bucket down and get his water. It was quite a ways down to the shore, and they had just had the Fourth of July. Well, it seems that Lawrence or Luther had an extra firecracker, and they hid it in the schoolhouse seat. So when they saw Manley getting ready to go down and soak his feet, one of them lighted it and the other threw it out the window, and it landed right beside Manley and went off. He began to screech, 'I've been shot, I've been killed.' It busted up the school, and all the kids ran out to see what happened to Manley.

"Isn't that a riot of a story?" Dorothy pauses for a few minutes and I gratefully sink back in my chair. I can see that she is thinking about where to go next. These little reprieves help both of us sort through her past and illuminate life in the village. Dorothy loves these stories and rightly so—they are funny and instructive. I ask her if there were any stories about tragedies in the village, thinking that I would get some historical tales of shipwrecks and men lost at sea. She shrugs her shoulders, squints, and looks at the ceiling.

"We had a few other things happen—little tragedies like drowning and fires and things. One of them is kind of a mystery. You might like this story, except that I have it all settled. [Dorothy had solved the mystery, at least to her own satisfaction.] Well, Walter Flye, Harry's son, was working with Ernest Marsh down on the bridge. There used to be a channel that they had to keep open so the scows could come up the river, and sometimes the men had to fix things. The story goes that Walter had married someone who had had a husband before. She was kind of racy, I think. Her first husband fell overboard in Bath and drowned. She married Walter, and his parents didn't approve of her, not one bit. But it didn't matter much, because they both died one after the other, soon after Walter was married. Some people thought that Walter's wife had managed to see to it that her mother-in-law didn't last too long after her husband's death.

"Anyway, Walter was working down on the bridge, and Ernest claims that he heard a splash behind him and Walter had fallen in the river. He wasn't conscious for Ernest to get him out or anything. He just fell in the river and didn't struggle, so Ernest couldn't rescue him.

"I have it all settled, and it is as simple as it can be, but the story doesn't go nicely with the history. I say that

Man and child on the King's Highway, looking north toward Alna and the Golden Ridge

E. Joseph Leighton photograph, Ivan Flye Collection

Ernest—and he could be kind of clumsy—got a big plank and had it long-ways on that ramp. He didn't realize it, but he knocked Walter overboard into the river. They all said that Walter died and couldn't be rescued, but that he had been home for lunch and probably his wife had poisoned him. Oh, that story was something. I was too young to be listening, but you don't miss much when you have friends that have older brothers listening at the dinner table at night. You find out an awful lot of things. They thought that Gert[10] had given her husband something, and that is why he fell over and drowned.

"I have always maintained that it would be simple enough for Ernest to swing around with that long plank in that little narrow place and hit him. He wouldn't even know he hit him. Walter went into the channel, and that was it. That is one of the stories that is in Sheepscot. You can see it was a busy place.

"You know, my father was justice of the peace, and there are all sorts of stories around that.[11] There was this old widower who was living all alone down on the family homestead, and he was some lonely. So he decided that he needed a wife, and he wrote away for one.[12] Now Pa told him, 'Joe if you get a wife, I will marry you for free.' That seemed like a good idea. I remember it was wintertime. We heard a knock on the door, and I looked out the window. Here was this sleigh with two people in it. They were right in the dooryard and had driven up on the snow—horse, sleigh, and all. He was there for my father to marry them. They had come from New York or somewhere in one of those matrimonial things. She was dressed in a lace curtain or something that she had wrapped herself up in.

"Pa told mother she would have to be a witness. She said, 'You got yourself into this, now get yourself out. I will have nothing to do with this business.' She was in the kitchen getting dinner. You know what he had to do?

"He took the two of them into our front parlor. In the corner was this two-seater divan. My father took this two-seater divan and put it against the fireplace. I think he was making kind of a ceremonial place for this wedding by rearranging the furniture, which wouldn't please my mother. My crippled sister Gladys and I were the witnesses to that wedding. I wasn't but ten years old, but Gladys was almost seventeen, so I guess she counted as a witness. Oh, yes, people were always getting married by my father.

"We had an old man who worked for us named Eddie Harrison. He was an Englishman, and some say he deserted from the navy. At any rate, he used to get drunk. One time when he had a little money, he went up to Lewiston and came home with a French-Canadian woman. Pa said to him, 'Where did you get her, Eddie?' 'Oh, Frankie, I got her off a druggist in Lewiston.' Evidently he went into a drugstore and said he needed a housekeeper and got this woman and brought her home. You know, that is all that I knew. We always called her his wife. She could hardly speak English. We'd go pick blueberries and things like that for them. Eddie had her supposedly as a wife, but you know, until I read Pa's diary I didn't know the whole of it. I discovered that he had taken Eddie and that woman down to the Methodist minister that lived next-door in the parsonage and had a ceremony of some kind. Isn't that cute?"

I dutifully nod as Dorothy stops for just a few minutes. I make myself and her a cup of tea. In the time it takes to boil the water the conversation takes another turn.

"These young girls that come in here and take care of me don't know a thing about Sheepscot. They all think that it is this little town where nothing ever happened. Did you know that the Underground Railroad went close to here? It went right up by Pemaquid. I remember my father took me down there for a picnic. We had the first Ford in Sheepscot, and Pa always drove it like it was a team of horses. He would say 'Whoa' when he wanted to stop and cluck his tongue when he wanted to go forward. He hated cars and always preferred a team of horses. Anyway, after haying, we always went on a picnic. Sometimes we would take a day trip and a picnic lunch. This time he took me down to Pemaquid in the car and showed me this barn. It was way down in the bottom of a field—close to the water, but you couldn't see the water from it. He said that it was part of the Underground Railroad—that the ship captains from Sheepscot and around were sympathetic, and they would let the slaves get on the ships in the South and would take them up the coast.[13] The barn was right tight to the water, so the slaves could get off without being seen and then stay in the barn until it was time to go to Canada. They would be passed along and along until they got away. My pa told me that and showed me the place. Do you know where it is? If I could get out of this chair, I could show you.

"I have one more story for you. You know I said that Grampa traded with everyone. Well, one day this black fella came into the store. Some thought he was descended from a slave because his name was Freeman, and some thought he had come up from Boston. At any rate, he had a very young wife, and Grampa took an interest in him. Grampa was an abolitionist and a sympathizer. The man said he could work if only he had a pair of oxen. He had saved enough money for one ox and could Grampa loan him money for another ox? Well, Grampa did. Time went by and time went by, and one day the man came back into the store and said, 'Squire Carney, I have some good news and some bad news for you. I got a pair of oxen, but your ox died.'

"Now that's just the way of it, Sheepscot, when I was coming along. Yessuh, quite a place it was."

Dorothy stops speaking and leans back in her chair with her usual expression—a mix of anticipation for my response and a slightly quizzical look. I tend to forget that she is well over ninety, and that this level of remembering—exhausting work for a young person—is even more so for someone who is almost a hundred. Dorothy is well aware that time is running out, and she often asks me when I will be done and if she will see this material written up. She does not find her present state of affairs particularly pleasant and says so. "This is the hardest part, waiting to die. It is all over. I am finished. I can't do anything, and I am no good to anyone." I keep reassuring her that I will write as fast as I can. I remind her that she has to stay alive long enough to get down all her stories. I promise to send her bits and pieces as they take shape. I am painfully aware that I am at sea in someone else's life and that, for all intents and purposes, Dorothy is relying on a stranger to tell the story of that life and to tell it in a way that is true to the past as well as to her perspective.

There is a sense of urgency on her part to pick only the best stories, the ones that are most illustrative of what

Sheep at Two Rivers Farm

she believes to be important about life in Sheepscot and life in general. Before this session, Dorothy had written down on the back of an envelope some notes to remind her of stories she wanted to tell me. This is no mean feat, as writing is nearly impossible because of her arthritis. The fact that she has made the effort is indicative of how important this is to her and how much she wants to get it right. Dorothy is clear that she is laying down not only her own story but also that of her village, and she is aware that almost no one else knows these tales; without her, they will vanish. They are as fragile as the spider webs that span the grass on a summer morning, and they weave a web of talk and action that captures, in Dorothy's words, "the way of it."

This particular set of stories begins to flesh out the complexities of village life and peoples the Sheepscot landscape with a whole new cast of characters. These are lean, tidy narratives with clear beginnings, middles, and ends. Dorothy's ability to deliver them whole comes from a life steeped in the oral tradition and frequent practice as a listener and a narrator. The characters are rich because their dialogue is so spare and their actions so understated. Their humor is dry as dust and their wit acerbic. These are stories without frills or fluff, and they serve a purpose beyond entertainment. They are part of the community web of talk that maintains social order, illuminates a collective mindset, and provides a glimpse of a world parallel to that of the historical record.

There are many lessons to be learned in this world,

and advice is quickly given. Family feuds are common-place and nothing to worry about. Belligerency is a personal and creative undertaking, a timeless and egalitarian method of settling or fueling disputes. Talking about these events sets a standard for fairness and proposes a template for acceptable behavior. Each person has a role that he or she can be counted on by the neighbors to play to perfection. The Flyes, for example, are notorious for their orneriness. Albion's barn really does eclipse his back-yard, and the effort it took to line it up perfectly with Harry's view from Dyer's Neck is a testament to the brothers' ingenuity and effort in thwarting one another.

As the stories unfold, the listener is secretly pleased by Mrs. Flye's tart comment at the sight of her husband's faulty embalming. "Conquered at last, Mr. Flye" suggests that he got what he deserved, with no sympathy on her part. Horace Marsh playing undertaker while three sheets to the wind is funny and, from our perspective, impossible to imagine. This little vignette takes the sting out of death and relegates it to a level of dark humor that is more satisfying than threatening.

Anonymity is in short supply in Sheepscot, Maine. The level of community intimacy serves as a method of keeping track of the actions of others and, in some cases, helping them to conform to the social order. Clearly Pa, as justice of the peace and a strong Methodist, did not encourage keeping company. Getting a wife from a drug-store in Lewiston is not nearly as spectacular as remaining unmarried. Mother's refusal to come out of the kitchen for the wedding of the old widower and his mail-order bride has more to do with her disapproval of the event's timing and spontaneity than it does with the event itself.

Dorothy's story about Walter Flye is also about the role of gossip. She exonerates Walter's wife as the possible perpetrator of the crime of killing Walter. To her, it is an accident pure and simple; yet there is a shadow cast on Gert, who was "married before" and described as "racy." It makes a better story when the facts remain shrouded in mystery; it also indicates that there was something about Gert that rubbed folks the wrong way. She will always be remembered as something other than what she probably was—if she is remembered at all.

Values come through clearly. It is important to tell the truth, and stories need to be based on fact—hence the reference to Lawrence Averill, who became a preacher and whose version of events can therefore be relied on. That what he says is true is also reflected in the phrase, "That is the truth that I've got"—implying that truth is simultaneously fixed and flexible. The fact that Lawrence scared the living daylights out of Manley Sargent is entirely irrelevant. This is not a mean-spirited act; rather, it is part of what constitutes humor. Mr. Sargent could have been injured, but again, that is beside the point. He wasn't—and all the kids in Sheepscot benefited when they took off from their studies to "see what was going on."

The Sargent brothers themselves are characterized as bright but peculiar. Their idiosyncrasies, such as the two doors leading into their house,[14] are offset by their talents as builders and inventors. Behavior is the standard of character. If you want to know what someone in Sheepscot is like, listen to the stories about them. Description and identity are embedded in action and in the collection of tales that surround the individual.

The story of the Underground Railroad and the companion piece about the ox and the young black man reveal another aspect of Sheepscot specifically and Maine in general. The Underground Railroad did exist in this part of central Maine,[15] although it is difficult to pinpoint the Pemaquid location to which Dorothy refers. Maine ship captains routinely transported runaway slaves up the coast and, later on, to Canada. Maine, which was originally part of Massachusetts, was one of the first states to outlaw slavery. As Bill Peterson, a maritime historian and boat designer said, "By virtue of its maritime history, Maine was always conservative and ahead of its time simultaneously. Once at sea, there was almost no one that would stop a vessel. This coastline has so many nooks and crannies that it is perfect for smuggling people, booze, and just about everything else."[16]

The story of the ox lifts the corner of the page of a little-known history in the community and at the same time says something about trading across cultures and class. Sheepscot and the surrounding towns of Damariscotta Mills, Bristol, and South Bristol each had a fledgling black community that, in some cases, dated back to the Revolution.[17] These little communities consisted mostly of farmers and laborers, but on the coast a large majority—almost half of all black men—were involved in the maritime industry.[18] The vital records of Newcastle indicate that there were small groups of black mariners,[19] some shop owners—such as a tailor and a watch cleaner—and a few quite well-to-do landowners.[20] Although African Americans living in Maine have never accounted for more than about 1 percent of the population, their history here is a rich one.

Mr. Freeman, the young black man of Dorothy's story, was born September 3, 1820.[21] His family moved to Sheepscot from Bowdoin only a few years before Grampa's family came from Boston. It is conceivable that Sanford Freeman, if he went to school at all, attended the same school as Grampa and, as they were fairly close in age, they probably knew one another. Sanford and his father, Anthony Freeman, bought two adjoining parcels of land from Sara Kennedy, one in 1850 for $44.00 and the other in 1859 for $66.00.[22] These two parcels were combined and appear on the maps of old Sheepscot as the Freeman farm. Sanford's great-grandfather may have been a slave brought here from the West Indies, and that piece of information found a convoluted way into the story.

A very early history of the area by David Quimby Cushman implicates a Captain Brown from Damariscotta as the first person to bring a slave, Black Nancy, to Maine. There is some confusion here, as slavery was outlawed in 1783 by a decision of the Massachusetts Supreme Court stating that the "free and equal" clause of the state constitution made the practice of slavery illegal. The story of Black Nancy in Cushman's history may be mixed up with stories about other slaves, or it may represent an amalgam of vignettes.[23] Slavery in Maine, although it existed as early as 1663, was generally attributed to the "trappings of a few of the gentry," and the slave population never exceeded five or six hundred.[24]

The census indicates that several free black families lived in Lincoln County from as early as 1790. The record of deeds mentions a Caesar Freeman, identified in the census as black, buying and selling land in Bath valued at several hundred dollars in 1801.[25] There is evidence in the town reports that occasionally these folks fell upon hard times and ended up on the pauper's list.[26] Some appear in the death notices and others, such as Sanford's brother, vanish altogether.

I am struck, as always, by how easily a life disappears from the historical record. After extensive research in archives in Maine and New York and many miles logged in cars and airplanes, the most I could discover about Jefferson Freeman, the youngest brother of the owner of the ox, is that he died on Staten Island in November 1845. What he was doing there is a matter for speculation. The best guess is that he found work among the oystermen and the thriving community of black fishermen on Staten Island. He may have decided that Sheepscot was too small a place and, like Huck Finn, he struck out for the territory ahead. Although he died at the age of only twenty, there is no official cause of death recorded. His older brother, Sanford, died of a carcinoma of the mouth on November 7, 1897. The attending physician is the predecessor of the doctor that delivered Dorothy. The story of black Americans in Sheepscot, Maine, is not an obvious one. In fact, this reference of Dorothy's is one of the only indications that they existed at all.

I return to Sheepscot on a typical March day. A light snow has fallen the night before; it is maple syrup season, which means that spring can't be too far off. The sun is warm and the sky blue. I stand on the bridge and count a handful of cars swishing through the slush on their way to somewhere else. The tide is out on the river and there are no traces of the wharves and shipyards that once lined its shores. It is quiet, almost deserted, and strangely lifeless—a far cry from the world portrayed in Dorothy's stories.

Sheepscot, looking north toward Alna and the Golden Ridge. Two Rivers Farm is at the upper right.
IVAN FLYE COLLECTION

1 Staff writer, "Sheepscot Woman Preserves Homes for Posterity," *Lincoln County News,* Sept. 1963. Retrieved March 15, 2003, from miscellaneous file box, genealogy and local history room, Wiscassett Library The article names a mysterious woman, Miss Pauline Fenno, who came to Sheepscot to buy up old houses and preserve them. A photo caption reads, "Alone on a high ridge right, overlooking the Dyer River, stands the Harry Flye house. It has been unoccupied for a long time, unless you count 'the hermit' who called it home until he disappeared as silently as he came."

2 Albion Flye, Last Will and Testament, *Vital Records,* Wiscasset, Maine, lists Edwin Flye's address as King's Highway in Sheepscot, the same street where Grampa Carney's house was located.

3 *Vital Records,* Newcastle, Maine. Wash Houdlette refers to Captain Washington Houdlette.

4 *Vital Records,* Newcastle, Maine. Albion Flye's wife was Annie S. Flye, born on Prince Edward Island. Albion died September 23, 1908. It was not uncommon in the early part of the century to have designated "hospice" folks who saw to the dying of local community members. It was often a neighbor or a close friend, or it could be simply the person designated for the job by the rest of the community.

5 *Maine Register, State Year-Book and Legislative Manual,* no. 39, June 1908, advertisement for Fred Harrington, funeral director and casket dealer in Damariscotta, Maine. Fred Harrington was the funeral director of choice for much of Sheepscot at the time.

6 Albion Flye, Last Will and Testament, *Vital Records,* Wiscasset, Maine. Regardless of the stories surrounding the animosity of the Flye family and the chilly relations between Mrs. Flye and her husband, Albion's will suggests that the bridges had been repaired. The executor of his estate was his brother Edwin, and Annie received a small percentage of his estate. Curiously, he left bonds of the Republic of Mexico, several which were valued at $2,425—a sizable sum in 1908. He also left a Home Savings Account of $1,600, hay worth $240, a horse valued at $40, a grocery wagon assessed at $20, and a sleigh worth $5. His estate, minus his farm and his bonds, came to a total of $360 as goods and chattel. The recipients of his wealth were his brother Edwin and his wife Annie.

7 Author's interview, Linwood Gamage, shipbuilder, August 15, 2001, South Bristol, Maine. In all likelihood, Mr. Sargent did not literally chop up his boat but probably modified it, either by shortening it or lengthening it. Horace Beck, *Folklore and the Sea* (Philadelphia: J. P. Lippincott, 1957). Wooden boat building was a time-consuming process, done largely by eye with the builder's own tools,

many of which he had made himself. All vessels, whether large or small, were considered something to be very proud of, and it is unlikely, therefore, that Mr. Sargent would destroy his boat; rather, he would tweak the design to make improvements.

8 F. Wendroth Saunders, "Maine's Valley of the Sheepscot," *Ford Times* (vol. 51, no. 2, February 1959), pp. 19–23. Retrieved from the vertical file, Maine Historical Society. This story appears almost verbatim in the Ford Motor Company publication. Dorothy was very good friends with the author. Given her propensity for the oral tradition, it is likely that this story was one of many that swirled around Sheepscot. We do know, however, that the Sargent brothers lived in Sheepscot and that their reputations were based on fact. The "facts" may have grown larger than the men themselves, but all of these stories arose out of actual events in the community.

9 Lawerence Averill was a teacher and a doctor of psychology. He was also a Methodist minister and preached in the Sheepscot church. His importance in the community is evidenced by the number of times he is mentioned in newspaper articles and even in an address made by Teddy Marsh on Sept. 3, 1956, as part of her introduction to Senator Margaret Chase Smith.

10 Brides Index, Maine State Archives, 1892–1955. Gertrude married Walter Flye of Alna on September 23, 1916, and then married James Clark of Franklin on Oct. 1, 1921.

11 *Maine Register, State Year-Book and Legislative Manual*, no. 47, 1916, lists F. I. Carney as Justice of the Peace, Notary Public.

12 Picture brides were not an uncommon occurrence, and references can be found as early as 1857 in the *New York Times*. Helen Bullitt Lowry, "Here Comes the Picture Bride," *New York Times*, March 13, 1921: BRM8.

13 William Peterson. Interview. Maritime history at Pemaquid. South Bristol, Maine, October 20, 2002.

14 I visited the Sargent house in Sheepscot in July 2003. The two entrances are identical. It is impossible to tell which is the "front door."

15 Underground Railroad Task Force, *The Underground Railroad in New England* (American Revolution Bicentennial Administration, Boston 200, 1976).

16 Philip W. Conkling, *From Cape Cod to the Bay of Fundy: An Environmental Atlas of the Gulf of Maine* (Cambridge, Massachusetts: MIT Press, 1995), p. 21. There are approximately 7,500 miles of coastline in the State of Maine, much

of it inlets and coves that are perfect for smuggling contraband.

17 United States Census of 1790 lists twenty-seven men in Maine as Free Blacks who headed families that totaled around a hundred members.

18 Jack Salzman, David Smith, Cornel West, ed., *Encyclopedia of African-American Culture and History* (New York: Macmillan Library References, 1996), vol. 3, pp. 1678–80.

19 William Pierson, *Black Yankee: The Development of an Afro-American Sub-culture in 18th-Century New England* (Amherst, Massachusetts: University of Massachusetts Press, 1988).

20 Christine Huston Dodge, ed., *Vital Records of Old Bristol and Nobleboro in the County of Lincoln.* Vertical file, Skidompha Library, Damariscotta, Maine. Although there are many mistakes in this work, Dodge does list in conjunction with the census small numbers of black families living in the area. The earliest deeds and records indicate a Boston Miller (Negro) taxed for 1 house and 100 acres of land in Bristol. There is a Boston Brackett, who was born in 1799 and died in 1882 and is buried in the Bristol Mills Cemetery. There are others as well, including Herbert Cuff and his sister, and the Freeman families, headed by Anthony Freeman and later Sanford Freeman. Both men married Caucasian women, who are listed in the census as white or mulatto, depending on the dates. Anthony married Rachel Lee from Bath and Sanford married Mary E. Carpenter from Newcastle. Their intention to marry was posted on May 26, 1856 (Newcastle Town Records, Marriage Intentions, 1835–91), p. 86. Mary was only sixteen at the time and Sanford was thirty-six. Mary died at the age of thirty-nine. There is a Charles Miller, born Aug. 25, 1850, and died Aug. 11, 1905, who is listed as watch cleaner and is buried in the Bristol Mills Cemetery. Sanford Freeman's sister, Julia, married into this same family.

21 State of Maine, Certified Abstract of a Certificate of Death lists Sanford's birth date and his mother's maiden name as Rachel Lee. The attending physician is A. M. Card.

22 Deeds, Lincoln County Court House, Wiscasset, Maine. Kennedy to Freeman, vol. 193, pages 572–73. The Freeman men bought and sold property in 1850 and 1853 and consolidated their holdings to Sanford in 1859.

23 David Quimby Cushman, *The History of Ancient Sheepscot* (Bath, Maine: E. Upton & Son, 1882), p. 157. This reference, however, is not collaborated. A "Black Nancy" does appear in Cyrus Eaton's *Annals of Warren* (Hallowell, Maine: Masters and Livermore, 1877), p. 535. She is Nancy Davis, who came to Warren, Maine, as a servant of the Dunbar family in 1785. She died, "very aged," on April 28, 1862. Also appearing in the *Annals of Warren* is a sad tale of Sallie Peters, "hardworking woman of the colored district," who froze to death in a wild northeaster on Jan. 16, 1861.

24 Jack Salzman, David Smith, Cornel West, ed., *Encyclopedia of African-American Culture and History* (New York: Macmillan Library References, 1996), vol. 3, p. 1679.

25 Deeds, Lincoln County Court House, Wiscasset, Maine. Hall to Freeman, "in consideration of 180 dollars paid by Cesar Freeman of Bowdoinham in the County of Lincoln and Commonwealth of Massachusetts...I convey unto the said Cesar Freeman a lot of land in said Bowdoinham containing 91 acres being lot number one of a tract of land surveyed for me by John Merril, Esquire, and part of a tract granted by the Plymouth Company to Edward Goodwin and conveyed by said Goodwin to me, J. Willis Hall." vol. 103, p. 44.

26 *Annual Report of the Town of Newcastle, Maine.* Sanford Freeman appears on the Paupers List with his mother Rachel. Another black family, Henry and Phillis Freeman, is listed as paupers. The estate of Phillis Freeman, vol. 268, is auctioned off to the inhabitants of Newcastle on May 20, 1886, for the sum of $239, which included land and some buildings. Phillis came upon this property at the death of her first husband, a Charles Stewart. Stewart bought the property in 1825 from a Mr. Kennedy and a Mr. Chase for a total of $59. As was often the habit of seafaring folk, they dreamed of a small farm as a respite from the dark waters and as a place for retirement. Unfortunately, Mr. Stewart did not get to retire—he drowned at sea. Phillis married Henry Freeman and within their lifetime lost the farm to taxes. In the 1860 census Henry is listed as black and Phillis is listed as a mulatto. Both are buried in the pauper section of the Sheepscot Cemetery.

Dorothy feeding Ramkin at the Captain's House, circa 1940
COLLECTION OF MARY ANN AND JOHN VINTON

Chapter Six

"NO ONE BELIEVED IT"
Leaving Home

*I*t was a long trip from North Carolina with endless airport delays and security checks. I had sent Dorothy a draft of some of the stories in hopes that she would approve of them and fill in details where I had written questions, and that we could move on to new topics. As usual, I sent her a few questions, mostly to do with ideas or themes that seemed to be emerging. They would serve as topics for our next visit. The airport was crowded, rental cars hard to find, but once I got out of Portland and headed toward Sheepscot I breathed a sigh of relief. As this process moved along, the visits with Dorothy felt like going home, our conversations between friends and across generations. I missed her and looked forward to her acerbic sense of humor and the sound of her voice. I arrive as usual, park the car, sprint up the stairs, and knock. I am grateful to find her tucked into her chair, my tea still in the cupboard, and the view from the window the same except for the season. It is a rainy November day, and the tide is half out on the river. The clam flats and the sky are the same color. It doesn't dampen her enthusiasm one bit. We haven't been seated for more than five minutes before she starts in.

"We all became something—that was what we were expected to do. My sister Doris went to school to become a teacher. Gladys, even though she was crippled, still went on to finish high school. My sister Alice went to Sargent's School of Physical Education, and I became a nurse. I was the only one who thought of it, and the others thought it was horrible.

"I always had my heart set on being a nurse. I had a neighbor, Harry Hall, who was a pal of my half-brother Richard, when they were young. He and his wife used to come down to Sheepscot in the summer, and she knew Newton Hospital in Newton, Massachusetts. She used to talk to me about it and had me write to them about the training. So I did, and they took me.

"They took me in the March class because I was too young for the fall. You had to be eighteen, and I wouldn't be eighteen until the winter, so I went in the spring class. There were eleven of us. I did three years at Newton and graduated from there, and during that time I did a stint at Children's Hospital in Boston. Children's was just getting going then, and it was quite something. All the nurses-in-training got shifted around. Some went off to the psychiatric wards, but I went to Children's.

"I wanted to get some money as soon as I was trained, so I signed up at our hospital to do private duty. My first job was an old man in Watertown. You had to have your uniforms, and you had to get yourself there. In those days you took the streetcar and walked and so on. I had night duty—that was from seven to seven. I had him for a few weeks, and then he got better.

"What happened next is an interesting story. No one believed that I would do this. After the old man, I needed a new job and signed up again. I got another job at the hospital. It was also night duty. It was an old lady—she had no use for me, and I didn't have any use for her. She had no use for anyone, for that matter. I was very unhappy.

"On the streetcar—which is how I got to the hospital—I happened to sit next to Grace Russell, who was one of the supervisors from our office. I always liked to be friendly, and so we would talk about one thing and another. On this day, she looked at me and said, 'Do you know anyone who would like to go to New Hampshire for the summer?'

"'Yes,' I said, 'I do.'

"'Are you sure?' she said.

"'Oh, yes,' I said. I would have done anything to get away from that woman!

"Well, my supervisor and I arranged that we would tell the hospital patient that I was called home for a family member, so that is how I got rid of her. Then I had a phone call from the new family, and the daughter, Mrs. Sampson, said that I was to go to North Station and get on such-and-such a Pullman car. I was not to wear a uniform, as I was going to the country where they wore only country clothes. I have forgotten what else the rules were, but she told me what seat to take on the Pullman and everything like that. Everyone was shocked. How could anybody go to New Hampshire without knowing anything about who you were working for or the conditions or where you were going to be? I said that I knew how to get home. I could walk, if I didn't like it.

"As it turned out, I was going to take care of Mr. Frank Webster, who at the time was head of Kidder Peabody in Boston.[1] He had had a stroke and needed private duty care. So I got on the train and headed for New Hampshire. We were met at the station by his chauffeur in a Rolls Royce, and I stayed on their estate on Squam Lake. I stayed with Mr. Webster until he died, and then I took care of Mrs. Webster until she died.[2] By then their daughter, Mrs. Sampson, who was a widow, had asked me to stay on and be her companion. So I said Yes, and I stayed with her. All told, I worked for them for seventeen years.

"Mrs. Sampson and I didn't miss a thing. I did the suggesting and she did the doing. We went everywhere. We went to Washington, D.C., and Florida. We went to Orlando. She had an open roadster. We sent the car down on the boat from Boston to Jacksonville, and we went down by train. We did everything. We went to the races at Daytona; we played golf every day. Neither one of us was very good at it, but we enjoyed it. The place in Orlando was a hotel where everyone knew everyone, and they visited and played cards in the evenings. Mrs. Sampson knew everyone and was liked by everybody. We took trips all around from there.

"One day we decided that we would drive across Florida to the west coast and then down the Tamiami Trail.[3] It was back in the thirties, so you can imagine the road. It was practically a dirt trail. It was nothing but a narrow road through a swamp. We would come to the bridges, which none of them could fit more than one car at a time. So we had to wait for people to pass. I was doing all the driving. I drove with a hammer on the floor under the front seat—just in case. When we stopped for gas in one of those little places in the middle of nowhere,[4] the man at the station noticed the hammer. 'Good idea.' he said. After all, we were two women alone with golf clubs in the back of this open car driving around. We visited Miami and West Palm Beach. We did the works.

"Mrs. Sampson was different, and she went her own way. She wasn't social and having tea parties. She could talk to everyone. We started to come to Sheepscot in the summer. She would come and visit Mother at the farm, and we didn't even have any indoor plumbing! She liked the neighbors and everyone liked her, so we just went there in the summers instead of New Hampshire. Life in New Hampshire was very formal, and the house was big, and you needed all kinds of help and things. Neither one of us liked it. So a little house came up for sale on the reversing falls on the Sheepscot River, and she bought it. It was called the 'Captain's House.' It was a tiny thing, but she fixed it all up and it was nice. There was a small vestibule and her room was downstairs with a bath. The second floor had a room that she reserved for her

The Captain's House

company or for me. She loved it up in Sheepscot in her house. I had a camp down on the river, but I could see that Mrs. Sampson needed something a little better than my camp, so this house turned out to be perfect.

"Once, when we were there during the war, we heard that the German submarines might be trying to land along the coast of Maine. They probably could, you know. We had neighbors from away—F. Wenderoth Saunders,[5] who was a painter, and his wife Polly, who was a singer. He was at Harvard or some such place. Anyway, I told Mary Ann Sampson and Dick Saunders about the possibility of the Germans' arrival. We decided that if

Kayaking at the Reversing Falls, 2005

they were coming to spy and things, and they were going to come up the Sheepscot River, that by golly, they wouldn't get far. So Dick and I got out some rifles. I had been given one as a present from Ross, and I think Dick Saunders had his own. At any rate, we decided to practice. So we went out along the river and had target practice. We figured we would shoot them before they shot us. I tell you, strange things went on in Sheepscot in the summer, but we didn't miss a thing.

"I stayed with Mrs. Sampson until it looked like the country was going to run out of nurses during the war and I would be drafted. Some of my friends from nursing school had already signed up. I decided to join the navy to be a navy nurse. At the time, they were sending all the nurses they could get their hands on to Hawaii, and they were gone for years. It looked like I would be going to Hawaii with everybody else, but I didn't get too far. I had this man from Sheepscot, Ross Chase, who had been my hero since childhood. He had been gassed and everything in the trenches during World War I. He decided that we needed to get married rather than have me go to Hawaii. Well, we did that. We just went to the chaplain and got married. Mrs. Sampson sent us beautiful flowers. No one came to the wedding because it was wartime, but after it was over, I was out of the service. I also left Mrs. Sampson at the same time. I got her another wonderful woman, Helen Bond, who was also from Sheepscot, and she stayed with Mrs. Sampson until she died.

"I have thought about this a lot. Who would have believed that I would have stayed on so long with this one family, just by being on the streetcar at the right time? It doesn't seem like much now, but in those days, New Hampshire was far away, and going to work for an unknown family was risky. I think I was lucky, but I also think that when something came my way, I took it and did something with it. I wasn't afraid to go after things. That is how I lived my life. Going with what comes and getting there. You have to.

"Well, that was that. Ross and I had Mary Ann and named her after Mrs. Sampson, who was delighted. After the war was over, we lived in Boston until my husband retired, and then we moved back to Maine. Ross loved Sheepscot and his family farm was up on Two Rivers. His father had died suddenly when Ross was five and didn't leave a will. That meant that the farm fell to his mother, Nora Ross, his brother, and his four sisters. Nora, because of the way the laws work, actually had an extra share of the property. She had one third and the other two thirds were divided up between all the children.

"Anyway, after he retired, he would spend his days in Sheepscot doing things around the farm. I never had to worry about how he was or if anything was wrong about the boat or anything. All the neighbors could look over

The Chase family at Two Rivers Farm, circa 1897.
Young "Ross" is the second from left.
E. Joseph Leighton photograph, collection of Doris Leighton Pierce

and see Ross, and they all knew him, if anything happened, they would call me.

"One day, Ross came home and said that the property was going to be up for sale. There was no one left, except for his brother out in Oregon and his sisters. He said, 'The girls have decided to sell home.' I couldn't sleep that night, because that place meant so much to Ross. I was awake all night. I said to myself, he has got to have his boat on the water, he has got to have this, and he has got to have that. I started going around all night long thinking about the neighbors or where there was water. It came to me that there was a place next to the cemetery.

"Ross always got up early and went fishing and then came in for breakfast. One morning, as we were sitting at the kitchen table, I said, 'Ross, would you mind living next to the cemetery?' He looked at me as if I had gone off my rocker. 'I know where there is a piece of land where you can have your boat when the girls sell the place.'

"The man who owned the land was a Carney like me. He came down from Grampa's brother, so we were cousins. He and Ross were of an age and had done things together when they were younger. I said to Ross, 'We are going down to see Bob Carney and see if he will sell us a piece of land so you can have your boat.' Immediately after breakfast, we went down and I told Bob Carney, 'Bob, the girls are selling the property, and you know what that will do to Ross. We have got to have a piece of land. Will you sell us some of the cemetery lots?' He said,

The Dyer River and the fields of Two Rivers Farm today

'I would sell it to Ross and no one else.' I asked him if he would sell us a piece for a garden and a piece that went down to the water. There was an old cellar hole in the front yard that had been bought by a neighbor. I asked Bob to see what he could do about that. So Bob went to see the girl who owned it and talked to her. She sold me the piece of land and didn't charge me too much, and we built our house there. That was how we solved that.

"I just couldn't let Ross go without a piece of Sheep-scot. After all, he and his family had been here from the beginning,[6] and it was his life. Selling home for Ross was like selling a piece of his life, he couldn't have lasted without a place to do the things he liked with the neighbors around. It wasn't right."

Dorothy does one of her famous pauses. I stop and try to redirect the conversation to a question I had asked much earlier when I discovered that she knew Lucy Farnsworth. Lucy is legendary in Maine and any story about her is worth listening to. I remind of her of Lucy, and her response is quick.

"You asked me about Lucy Farnsworth. Well, I knew her because my mother was Flora Sprague and her father was Elisha Sprague. His sister, Mary, married a Farnsworth. Aunt Mary was my mother's aunt. The Farnsworths were from down in Friendship. Lucy's father was a miser and so was Lucy. She was always honoring her father. I'll tell you a good one here.

"Aunt Mary used to come over to Sheepscot from Rockland to visit my mother, and one time, she invited my half-sisters to come back with her. They had a coach-man and carriage that would meet Aunt Mary and the girls when they got to the station. Well, Aunt Mary came home with the girls for an overnight visit. When it came time to go home, Lucy wouldn't let Aunt Mary have the carriage to take the girls back to the station. She made them walk, and it was far. That is how stingy she was. She was such a miser that she had all the burners on her stove blocked up but one so she could save money.

"Her father was a miser and mean, too. He used to run the waterworks in Rockland, and if he found anyone saving a pail of water to take home, he would do something about it. Oh, I tell you, they were something. My father used to go to Rockland on business, and my mother would go up and see Lucy from time to time. She would bring her cookies, and Lucy liked that. I remember going with her when I was little and sitting in the borning room, which is a little room in the back of the house, with Lucy eyeing me. At any rate, she honored her father. Her brother died, and Lucy inherited everything from everywhere. She and Aunt Mary used to have squabbles. Lucy, of course, never married; that might have taken money. She wore the same clothing for years and years until it dragged in the street. She even willed her old clothes to some distant relative out West. They, of course, didn't want all those rags that had been wallowing around out on the road.

"Well, I got word that Lucy had died. I was with Mrs. Sampson at the time. No one even knew she had died, except that she always ordered delivered a chicken heart or liver or milk for the cat every day, and it didn't get picked up for several days. So I guess someone went to see what the matter was and found her dead.

"Anyway, Mother went down to see about the house, and I came on to help her, as Mother wasn't well and shouldn't have been doing anything. I went down to Rockland with Mother, Uncle Will Sprague, and Cousin Hannah. Cousin Hannah was so excited about seeing the house that she put her hat on backside-to. We went in, and that house was filthy. There was a carpet on the stairway in the front hall, and it was stuffed behind each stair riser with letters and money that she was going to take upstairs with her when she got ready. The dining-room table was covered with letters. This was the house where she did her business. You know that she made a million dollars, and her house was just filthy, dust and dirt everywhere. There was a pail in the kitchen sink to catch water from a leaking faucet, because she was so stingy that she wouldn't get the washer fixed to stop the leak, and she figured she could reuse the water. She was smart, even cagey, but her hands were only for money. She even picked a bank to manage her affairs without letting on in the beginning to the bank who she was. I tell you she was a cagey one.

"Being the last of the family, we came up to Rockland to find her will and things. We couldn't go through the house and get started on packing up things and making the arrangements without the will. The chief of police followed us everywhere we went, up and down and around. Nosuh, we couldn't find the will. We decided it was down at the bank, so the chief of police and us, the relatives—old folks kind of stumbling around—went over to the bank. The will wasn't there, and we went back to Lucy's house upstairs to look around some more. There was a bureau in a closet in her bedroom, and here was the will. Well, then, no one wanted to read it. So we went down to the dining room and assembled there. The chief of police read the will to us. The only problem there was that he couldn't pronounce any of the words. So here we all were listening intently while the chief of police mumbled along, mispronouncing things—you could hardly understand what he was saying. It was hilarious.

"In that will were the directions for all the things she wanted done. One of them was to have the art museum honor her father. I tell you, if she came back now and saw what they have done to that art museum, all those people would be blown to Hell. She was specific, and it was very carefully spelled out what she wanted done.

"She owned the whole block, and she wanted the bottom floor to stay stores and pay rent and things, and the second floor was for business and offices, and the third floor was to be an art museum. She even had a picture of her father painted and hung there so you could see it when you came in. The art museum was to be on the third floor only. The bottom floors were to provide some income for the museum. Now it is all different. It looks to me that everyone who ever ran it got into making money and making a name for himself. Why, the museum has even gone on to expand. The stores are gone, and there are no offices. They are lucky that Lucy cannot come back. You know, they didn't even have the decency to maintain Lucy's grave. When she was alive, the family plot was beautiful. I knew about that, and I had a copy of the will. When I found that her grave was a mess, I threatened to raise a fuss and make them clean it up and keep it that way. Oh, I tell you, there is all kinds of history."

Dorothy's story of Lucy Farnsworth strikes a chord. Everyone in the state of Maine knows that "The

Farnsworth," as the museum is affectionately known, is synonymous with the paintings of N. C., Andrew, and Jamie Wyeth. One of the most famous, Andrew Wyeth's *Christina's World,* which hangs in the Metropolitan Museum of Art, is an American icon. As Dorothy talks, I am startled to realize that I have an instant and permanent image of Christina Olson but none of Lucy Farnsworth. In fact, I have never thought about her, let alone her father, until now.

The Farnsworth invokes many instantly recognizable images. There are new Wyeth exhibits[7] and a new Wyeth Center, as well as the Gamble Education Center, named after the generous and talented Edwin Gamble.[8] There is a gallery dedicated to Jamien Morehouse, the late wife of Philip Conkling, director of the Island Institute. Jamien Morehouse was a strong advocate of the institute, as well as island life. The gallery's opening exhibit, *On Island: A Century of Continuity and Change,*[9] was a testament to her indomitable spirit in the face of a losing battle with breast cancer, her love of the islands, her family, and Maine. The Farnsworth brings to mind a whole host of other events and activities common to a thriving and vital museum. However, it does not bring to mind images of Lucy Farnsworth or her father. I suspect that few visitors to the museum could locate the portrait of its founder.

Dorothy paints Lucy almost as deftly as Andrew Wyeth paints Christina. The latter makes her way painstakingly across a field full of hay stubble. Her print dress and twisted back are soaked in midsummer light. The ghost of a once prosperous New England farm limits her horizon. Like the museum and the painting, the Olson House,[10] located in nearby Cushing, attracts hundreds of tourists every year.

Lucy, on the other hand, is conjured up in shades of black and gray, making her unhappy way around the city of Rockland, hardly beloved by the citizenry. Dorothy is merciless in her description of this eccentric and mean-spirited old lady who orders chicken innards for her cat. Like the Olson house, the Farnsworth Homestead has also become a tourist destination.[11] However, it is more a monument to what money and historical preservation can achieve than it is to Lucy herself. Lucy's plan backfired: She and her father have taken a back seat to a poor, homely woman from Cushing, who has become a permanent fixture in the American psyche. The irony of this situation is exquisite and is not lost on Dorothy, one of only a handful of people still living who actually knew Lucy. It smacks of the same form of New England justice that was meted out to Mr. Flye. Fate, at least in the State of Maine, does not suffer the arrogant and self-serving lightly.

I am curious about Dorothy's life with Mrs. Sampson and her role as a companion. On the surface, they seem an unlikely pair; yet their friendship lasted a lifetime and obviously went beyond the typical employer-employee relationship. To this day, Dorothy's loyalty to Mrs. Sampson is steadfast. She talks about the times they spent together with great pleasure, and a studio portrait of the two women, heads together, that sits on Dorothy's bureau speaks for itself. When I ask her about this relationship, Dorothy says, "I was always honest, no fooling around. She could count on me to tell the truth and to make sure that things were done right. I took care of everything and acted as a go-between for her and other people. I paid her bills and everything. She liked the things I planned for us to do. We had quite a time together. I went right on seeing Mrs. Sampson after I was married, and I took my daughter Mary Ann to see her, too. I named her after Mrs. Sampson."

Webster's definition of a companion is "one employed to live with and serve another." This could not be further from the truth as a descriptor for their relationship. A better definition might be found in the proverb, "Choose the neighborhood before you choose the house; choose the companion before you choose the journey." Clearly, Mary Ann Sampson had chosen well.

Mrs. Sampson was born Mary Ann Messinger Webster, the only daughter of Frank Webster and Fidelia Messinger. As a child, she lived in an imposing house at 167 Commonwealth Avenue in the Back Bay area of Boston and summered on Squam Lake, where her father had a share in a large family estate. She was educated at Miss Ireland's School in Boston, a well-respected college preparatory institution, and despite being the child of wealth and privilege, she grew up to be slightly bohemian and avant-garde. With less than enthusiastic support from her father, Mary Ann married William Sampson, a New York stage actor, on August 29, 1900, in Newton, Massachusetts.[12] There were no wedding announcements in any of the papers, and the only place that her marriage is mentioned is in the City of Newton, Massachusetts, *Marriage Registry.* She was twenty-five at the time and he was forty-one, and it was a first marriage for both of them. Curiously enough, William Sampson was from Canton, Massachusetts, which was the birthplace of Mary Ann's father and the early home of her mother. The couple lived in New York and traveled extensively in Europe, despite her seasickness on the voyages coming and going. The Sampsons were part of the New York theater world until "Billy" Sampson died in New York City at the age of sixty-three in 1922. Mary Ann, then a relatively young widow, returned to Boston and moved in with her parents until they died. She never remarried and did not have any children.

After her mother's death in December 1932,[13] Mary Ann and Dorothy moved out of Boston to a much smaller and more ordinary house in Wellesley Hills, Massachusetts, that Dorothy found for them. It was during these years that Mary Ann and Dorothy traveled to Florida. In 1945 she and Dorothy became life members of the New England Historic Genealogical Society. She continued to be an active supporter of the theater arts as well as music, especially the New England Conservatory. Dorothy remembers her entertaining up-and-coming young actors and actresses as well as more established ones, such as Peggy Wood, who started out in silent pictures but was better known for her role as a nun in *The Sound of Music*.[14] Mary Ann Sampson attended theater openings and was active in the Unitarian church right up until she died on June 27, 1956, at her home in Wellesley Hills. She was attended by her minister and Helen Bond, also from Sheepscot.

There is not a great deal of information or memorabilia regarding Mrs. Sampson or her husband. Her great niece has a few old photos and remembers her great aunt as being "fun." When asked to elaborate, she said, "Oh, she used to make a store for the children under the table in the dining room." One photograph that is particularly telling is of the young Mary Ann sitting on a table on the porch of a New Hampshire cottage, swinging her feet. A tall, rangy young woman, she looks out of the photograph with a slightly cocked head and a bemused expression on her face. Another is a picture of Billy reading the paper while sitting in a rocking chair on a porch at Squam Lake. William Sampson is unquestionably a handsome man; he looks to be in his forties, and his open shirt collar and dark, slicked-back hair give him a slightly rakish air. Their marriage and life together, however, remain somewhat of a puzzle. As the photographs are from a family album, it is safe to assume that Billy Sampson came to the estate on Squam Lake from time to time in the summer, and yet virtually no one in the family remembers him. His only legacy, besides a few pictures, is a trunk full of old costumes that are squirreled away in the attic of a distant relative.[15] In fact, in the whole time Dorothy was with Mrs. Sampson, she never remembers seeing a picture of him or hearing any stories about him. Billy Sampson, regardless of his career on the stage in New York, remains largely a mystery.

Both of these women, each in her own way, were ahead of their time. Dorothy's history in Sheepscot of "tooting around" with the neighbors prepared her to snap up the opportunities that life presented to her—or, in her words, "going with what comes and getting there." The "getting there" is an interesting process, combining Dorothy's spirit of adventure, strong sense of roots and place, outrageous sense of humor, and the need to make things right. She attributes her ability to take risks and make the most of situations to her upbringing and early life in the village. As she says repeatedly about her spur-of-the-moment decision on the streetcar, "No one believed I would do such a thing." It was a far-from-conventional choice—as unconventional as two women driving alone in an open roadster across Florida with a hammer for protection.

Mary Ann Sampson found a unique friendship in this funny, independent young woman from Maine and an unlikely "home" in Sheepscot. The house she bought and fixed up is modest by any standards. It was probably built in the late 1700s and, at the time she bought it, needed quite a bit of work. The end result was clearly worth it, as the view of the reversing falls is lovely, open and full of light. The little cape is located across the bridge in Alna, and it is in plain view of almost everyone in the village. It is about as far from a formal, private house on a family compound in New Hampshire as one can get, and she kept it right up until her death in 1956.

The painter F. Wenderoth Saunders and his wife Polly lived just down the street. His oils and watercolors hang in practically every house in Sheepscot and Mrs. Sampson's was no exception.[16] This community attracted authors, preachers, painters, and the like, a lively and eclectic group.

Life was good for this wealthy, solitary woman who came alone to Sheepscot in the summertime. The neighbors accepted her idiosyncrasies in the same way they accepted those of the Sargent brothers, the Flyes, or "Teddy" Marsh; they allowed her to be who she was. But she is remembered best and more dearly by Dorothy and her daughter than by anyone else, including the members of her own family. In sharp contrast to her mother's obituary, which takes up an entire column in the *New York Times,* Mary Ann's obituary in the Boston *Globe* is a tiny entry in the alphabetical death list; the one in the Wellesley *Townsman* states that, "She leaves no close relatives." Considering the size and power of the Webster clan, this is an odd statement. Mary Ann's brother Edwin Webster was one of the founding partners of Stone and Webster, a construction company that, at the time of his death on May 10, 1950, had done $2 billion worth of business, including the Oak Ridge Atomic Laboratory.

T'other side of Sheepscot

He was on the board of trustees for the Massachusetts Institute of Technology as well as the United Fruit Company. Mr. Edwin Webster had four children, all of whom were alive at the time of Mary Ann's death. Yet Mary Ann appears to sink from her family's surface without a ripple.

As Dorothy says, "Mrs. Sampson liked the neighbors and they liked her." Although her arrival in Sheepscot was largely a matter of happenstance, the ties that Mary Ann Sampson formed there were lifelong and in many ways appear stronger than those with her family's home in New Hampshire. Like Dorothy, Sheepscot offered a way of life to Mary Ann Sampson, one that suited her and gave her a sense of place on her own terms.

On a sunny summer afternoon many months later, I am able to locate Mary Ann's old house, remembering from an earlier conversation Dorothy's description of the view from the dock, which looks right down the Sheepscot. The view has probably not changed much since Mary Ann lived here forty years ago. I knock on a neighbor's door and ask about the house. The woman who answers has lived in the village for generations and remembers Mrs. Sampson, whom she describes as someone who "kept to herself in later years—nice woman—a good neighbor."

1 " F. G. Webster Dead; A Boston Banker; Senior Partner of Kidder Peabody & Co, dean of the city's financiers. Fought in the Civil War. Began career in a book bindery—contributed liberally to Boston Philanthropies." Special to the *New York Times*, Jan. 23, 1930, p. 20.

2 "Mrs. Frank G. Webster, Widow of Senior Member of Kidder Peabody and Company," *New York Times* obituary, December 17, 1932. "Mrs. Webster lived at 167 Commonwealth Avenue, Back Bay. She is survived by two sons, Laurence J. Webster and Edwin S. Webster, vice president of Stone and Webster, both of this city, and a daughter, Mrs. William Sampson, who made her home with her mother."

3 Frank Stockbridge and John Perry, *So This is Florida* (New York: Robert M. McBride & Company, 1935), pp. 144–45. The Tamiami Trail, which opened in April 1928, traverses the Everglades. It is 200 miles long, and the name is derived from Tampa and Miami. The Everglades became a national park in 1934, about the time that Dorothy and Mrs. Sampson were driving through. It is described in this early travel guide as "the last great area of America's primeval frontier.... On the banks of the rivers and lakes are to be found the rookeries of countless thousands of birds, among which are many forms of herons, white egret, scarlet and white ibis, and that now most rare of beautiful birds, the roseate spoonbill.... Alongside the Tamiami Trail runs a wide canal.... Here the traveler has his easiest opportunity to observe the Florida Alligator at close range. The huge lizards, seldom more than nine or ten feet long, may occasionally be seen swimming or floating in the water with only their elevated nostrils and eyes visible above the surface."

4 National Scenic Byways Program, *Tamiami Trail Scenic Highway* www.byways.org/travel/byway.html, March 25, 2003. Here Dorothy is referring to what was known as a "way station." These were the first buildings along the route and were built to assist motorists. They are the equivalent of the old-fashioned filling station. They did sell cold drinks, a little food, and a few supplies.

5 F. Wenderoth Saunders was a longtime summer resident of Sheepscot. A graduate of Harvard University, he was an author and illustrator who taught at the Fessenden School in Boston. He wrote and illustrated several children's books, including one about the Brooklyn Bridge. He died in 1991 at the age of ninety-two.

6 David Quimby Cushman, *The History of Ancient Sheepscot and Newcastle* (Bath, Maine: E. Upton & Son, 1882), p. 365. Captain Chase was one of the first settlers of Sheepscot.

7 Farnsworth Art Museum and Wyeth Center. "We Are the Farnsworth" (August

15, 2003). Website for the Farnsworth Art Museum: www.farnsworthmuseum.org

8 Edwin Gamble exhibit at the Farnsworth Museum website www.tfaoi.com/ newsmu/nmus36n.htm, August 15, 2003. This website gives a brief description of the Gamble exhibit and a biography of the artist and his work. October 12, 1997–January 4, 1998, exhibit dates.

9 Farnsworth Art Museum exhibit, *On Island: A Century of Continuity and Change, June 25–October 15, 2000* The catalogue for this exhibit includes an introduction and tribute to Jamien Moorehouse. It is poignant and insightful, giving the reader another glimpse of "Maine, the way life should be."

10 Farnsworth Art Museum and Wyeth Center, "General Information," www.farnsworthmuseum.org/general/olson.html, August 15, 2003.

11 The Farnsworth Homestead is located adjacent to the museum. The interior has been completely re-done in a fashion that would fit the times, but probably did not fit Lucy. The flyers at the door explain the restoration process. The kitchen is as Dorothy describes it, complete with the one burner available on the stove.

12 City of Newton, Massachusetts, *Marriage Registry,* vol. 501, p. 531. New England Historic Genealogical Society, letter to author, August 14, 2003. "We

looked in vain for a newspaper article about their marriage. Three papers were current in Newton at the time…one carried an announcement. Neither did the Boston *Globe* or the Boston *Evening Transcript*. It became apparent that we were at the point of diminishing returns and stopped searching further."

13 Obituary of Mrs. Frank G. Webster, *New York Times*, December 17, 1932.

14 Doug Macaulay, *Great Character Actors,* July 1, 1988, www.dougmacaulay.com/kingspud/sel_by_actor_index Peggy Wood was born in Brooklyn in 1892. She began her work in theater at the age of eighteen in *Naughty Marietta*. She appeared on television as the mother in *I Remember Momma*. Her final film was *The Sound of Music* in which she played the Mother Abbess. She died of a cerebral hemorrhage on March 18, 1978, in Stamford, Connecticut, at age eighty-six.

15 John Drew, *My Years on the Stage* (New York: E. P. Dutton & Company, 1922), p. 100. There is a reference here to William Sampson being cast as Dull, the constable, in Shakespeare's *Love's Labor's Lost,* in which he appeared with John Drew, who had the lead.

16 Conversation with Edna Verney, Sheepscot, Maine, July 30, 2003.

"What a beautiful day."

Chapter Seven

FINAL LEE
Observations on Old Age

When I am in Maine during the summer, I visit Dorothy at least once a week. I leave drafts of her stories for her to read, and she goes through them with a fine-toothed comb, making notes here and there when something is inaccurate or in need of more detail. Our routine includes a cup of tea, some cookies, and at least an hour-long chat. On this particular day, near the end of my stay, I arrive as usual and find Dorothy looking pensively out the window. She seems a little quieter than normal and obviously has something on her mind.

"I told Mary Ann and John that I don't want a funeral. It would be a total waste of money. I told them that they can tell everyone in the family that these are my wishes and that is it. Funerals are ridiculous for people as old as I am. Most of my friends are dead, and it would mean that family would have to fly here from California and places, and you would have to come up here from North Carolina. I would rather everyone went out to lunch someplace. I also told them that they can do anything they want with my body. They can bury me anyway they want. When it is over, it is over.

"I don't have any regrets. I have had some disappointments—everyone does. But I don't have any regrets at all. I am so proud of my daughter, and I love my son-in-law—not many people can say that. What more could I ask? You live the life as it comes to you, but you pick what you think is best. You do that as best as you can. It is these people that sit back that I don't like. There is one girl who comes in here, and she is lazy. You call her in and ask her to do something for you, she will do it all right; but if there is a book on the floor that you are going to fall over, she won't pick it up. She just goes on her way. She is lazy. I couldn't look at that book without picking it up, knowing that someone might fall over it. You see what I mean.

"Hard work is important and trying to make good choices. And oh, yes, you have to be independent. You have to say what you think. If others don't like it, they don't have to have you. It is that simple. I think you have to live on your own, use your own thinking. You are here for a purpose, and you should show what you can do and what you can't do. You have to live and do things right and be happy about it.

"I'll tell you a little story. I was into genealogy. I was mixed up with the library—anything that I could do like that and I could be of help, I did it. I knew the woman who became secretary at the town hall. She was from Massachusetts, and she was breezy. She didn't care about knowing her neighbors. I knew that there were a lot of people in this area that needed genealogy, and it was my hobby. I knew that there were a lot of people who wrote to the town office and wanted to know about their ancestors. She would never answer their letters. So I went over and told her that if anyone wrote to her and asked questions about their family, and she didn't want to bother with it, give it to me. If they would send a letter with a stamped envelope, I promised to answer it. I knew she [the town secretary] would just tear it up anyway. So I wrote to these people.

"One day the telephone rang, and a woman in Grand Junction, Colorado, was on the phone. She didn't wait to write to me. She wanted to know about Captain Flagg down on the Boothbay Harbor Road. We talked, and I said that I would do what I could. She said she was coming East. I found out where he had lived on the River Road. I went around asking people questions. So I found out quite a lot. She and her husband came, and we had the best time together. I helped her so much. Captain Flagg was a very interesting person.

"It seems that Captain Flagg was a sea captain on the Damariscotta River. He went everywhere and did a lot with the China Trade. He got acquainted with some Russians on his travels. When the Chinese and Russians got into a fight, the Chinese closed harbors and rivers and things like that, and Captain Flagg found out that there was a Russian ship stranded in China on a river. The crew was starving. Captain Flagg got up the river and took them food and saved them. When the hassle was over and they could get the boat out, the Russians wanted him to come to Russia to be celebrated. He didn't go, but they gave him all kinds of things. They made a big deal over this guy. That was Captain Flagg, who was the ancestor of the girl who called.

"One day I got started up the road to Glidden Hill, and I saw an iron rod fence for a cemetery. I visited all cemeteries, and I had a feeling about this one. I stopped in front and started snooping around, and I saw Flagg on one of the tombstones, so I went in to investigate. It was Captain Flagg, the girl from Colorado's great-grandfather and great-grandmother. She came East to take a wash of that stone and to see me.

"I found a man who knew all about Captain Flagg, and he invited us in and talked to us about the captain. I went home and made him an apple pie. He was an old, old man and was delighted to have somebody come in and talk to him. So there you see, you take it all around. I was always doing something. Now I can't do anything. I can't write to my friends or talk on the phone, because I can't hear. Most people probably think I am dead.

"You know, you asked me about religion and church. It has dropped out of my life completely. It is interesting, though. My mother was a Congregationalist, and the church was open in the morning and again in the afternoon. The minister used to come from Newcastle in a horse and buggy and tie it up out back. My mother went to afternoon services. My father was a Methodist and so was Grampa. He and Colonel Murray paid for the church in Sheepscot, and Grampa founded the church camp in the summer. So I was brought up with the Congregationalists and the Methodists, and then I got sent to Hebron, which was Baptist. So I saw the Baptists for a while and looked them over. Then, when I was with Mrs. Sampson, we were Unitarians, but we didn't bother about church because there wasn't any right where we were. The help were all Catholics, and they always went to church every Sunday. When we moved to Wellesley, we went to the Unitarian Church to get acquainted with everyone. I went to the Unitarian Church with her every Sunday. So that was that.

"Then, after Ross retired and we moved back to Maine, I tried out the Episcopalians. I liked them well

The Valley Church

enough and got involved in the church. I was on the altar guild, treasurer, and all of that. When I went to Salt Lake with John and Mary Ann, I didn't do anything. But when I came back here, I tried to go back with the Episcopalians, but I couldn't stand all the newness of everything. I didn't know any of the people, and the rituals were all different. I had the old prayer book, and I used to go to the eight o'clock service. We were all standing around in a circle and having to shake hands with your neighbor in the middle of the service, and you were doing every damn thing that is peculiar. I just walked out. That was it.

"The assistant came over here to see me and asked if I wanted communion, and I thought it would be nice. But then I sat here and thought it over and called her up and told her to forget all about it. I realized that I had made a mistake. And doggone didn't she come anyway— but I still said, 'No thank you.' I am still getting all the monthly bulletins and things. I guess they are hopeful that I don't die a wreck.

"No, I am all done with churches. I think what matters is how you live. I think truth matters. We were raised that way; Mother wouldn't stand for anything but the truth. I think the other thing is to be thankful. I don't have to say a prayer or a certain thing. I just feel that if I am truthful and honest about things I do and be thankful for them and that is enough. At night I review my day, and I can say that I am thankful about this or that. That is all that matters. I don't have to have a religion that I have to argue about. Nosuh.

"You know that I am going to the Veterans' Home next Thursday at 9:30. That will be it for me. That is my permanent and last place. I have had a good old life. It is amazing what can go on in a life. You have to die someplace, and that is that. I am going to go there and read my favorite book, *Come Spring*. I am making the best of it, whatever it is that comes. There will always be something that you don't like, but Old Dorothy will have to make the best of it. It should be that way."

On the day that Dorothy moves to the Veterans' Home, I arrive at the nursing home early to visit a little and to say good-bye. The weather is nearly identical to what I remember of the day I first met her a year ago. Summer days in Maine are the great gift of the long winters. They are few and far between, which makes them even more precious. The tide on the river is in, the air as clear as window glass. Dorothy is sitting in her wheelchair in a flowered robe with all of her possessions packed around her in three plastic bags. She has been both organized and inventive, using the latest copy of *Down East* magazine as a sort of filing cabinet. She has put papers and photos that she doesn't want bent inside the magazine and then "taped" it up with elastic bands. She shows every sign of being, in her own words, "ready to go and see what comes next."

Her daughter and son-in-law are there, and they decide to drive to the Veterans' Home through Sheepscot, giving Dorothy a last look at the family homestead and the village. The van driver wheels her out of the assisted-living facility into the sunshine. This has the potential to be a very tearful and maudlin moment, but Dorothy will have none of it. Her friends come out to say good-bye and wish her good luck, knowing that she will not be back. She smiles, chats, and waves. As her wheelchair is lifted into the van, she looks up at the sky and over at the tidewater in the river and says, "What a beautiful summer day," and off she goes.

Dorothy died in October.

IN THIS LOVELY, POIGNANT BOOK, Bird Stasz writes: "The only place where Sheepscot exists, as Dorothy knows it, is in her memory." In one sense this is clearly true, but in another, it no longer is, for Bird Stasz has saved Dorothy's memories for posterity. In so doing, she has made them a permanent part of the collective consciousness of the Sheepscot community. The Dorothy who springs so vibrantly to life from these pages would have been delighted to know that her strongly held sense of place lives on for future generations to share.

The economic and social conditions that created the tight-knit village community that Dorothy describes in such sparkling and endearing detail are long gone. Meanwhile, the natural beauty of the Sheepscot Valley continues to draw people "from away," accelerating the process of gentrification that she laments. The sense of place that Dorothy personifies captivates these people and holds them. A number of the newcomers of Dorothy's time are now the ancestors of third-generation Mainers. They, and their descendants, have created a new set of shared memories that continues to sustain Sheepscot as a community.

In 1969 one of these families from away—the Barths—founded the Sheepscot Valley Conservation Association (SVCA). Aware that the wave of newcomers, of which they were a part, threatened to overwhelm the natural beauty and community values of the Sheepscot Valley, the Barths and their friends formed an organization with the mission of preserving the heritage of their new home.

In the decades since 1969 the increasing affluence and

mobility of Americans, combined with the virtual collapse of Maine's rural economy, have placed added strains on villages such as Sheepscot, especially those endowed with such spectacular natural beauty. Once the economic basis for a vibrant community has ceased to exist, it takes a conscious and deliberate effort to keep the community, and its sense of place, alive. SVCA, now headquartered in Sheepscot Village, is part of that effort.

SVCA engages in a wide range of activities, from traditional land trust activities to advocacy. To date, SVCA has protected 1,700 acres and 12 miles of riverfront through acquisition and conservation easements. The easements work together to protect the valley's rural character, some conserving working farms and forestlands, others protecting rare plants and wildlife habitat. SVCA maintains four public hiking preserves that hopscotch up the watershed, allowing the public to experience the changing character of the river from stream to wide estuary. The twelve-year-old water quality monitoring program relies on forty dedicated volunteers who monitor conditions for wildlife such as the federally endangered wild Atlantic salmon, and for human safety at the various swimming holes. The Association has also played a leadership role in a number of important issues affecting the river, from the licensing of a nuclear power plant in the 1970s to the recent discussions on the siting of a Wiscasset bypass. It has provided mapping services to local towns and nonprofit groups and has helped towns in the development of local comprehensive plans.

Today SVCA itself is an evolving community of over 500 families working together to sustain a sense of place in this marvelous valley. We are honored to be the sponsor of this delightful book. We hope you, the reader, will be inspired by it to join with us in working to fulfill our mission of "conserving the natural and historic heritage of the Sheepscot watershed."

Honor Fox Sage
President

BIRD STASZ is an associate professor at Elon University in Elon, North Carolina, where she teaches courses in education and documentary studies. She divides her time between North Carolina and South Bristol, Maine.